CYCLE / PSYCHO

PERSONALITY

CYCLE / PSYCHO

PERSONALITY

Many common criminals may not be aware of the concept "psychopath" while many well-dressed, well-mannered, and well-educated people may very well be aware of the concept and yet be in denial that their own cycle of behavior happens to exemplify the psychopath.

JVP
Published by
Jo-Val Publishing, LLC
Avon, Indiana

www.jvpublishers.com

1st Edition: Based on a Motivational Presentation Created by Brother S. A. Tinnin-Bey

Printed in the United States of America.

ISBN: 0-9629832-7-6 (soft cover)
ISBN: 0-9629832-8-4 (hard cover)

This book is printed on acid-free paper.

"Cover illustration by Rodney Ross

E-mail Address: stinninbey@yahoo.com

~~~

"I would like to dedicate this book to my late parents, Richard A. and Betty L. Tinnin, to my grandparents, Prophet and Lillian Curtis, who all modeled the principles of righteousness; and the honorable leaders in the close knit family I was blessed with."

~~~

This book relates a true story based on events, which occurred in the life of a person who had a repetitious cycle of counter-productive thinking and behavioral patterns, extending from childhood into adulthood. Consequently, this person suffered multiple incarcerations, which culminated in what is defined as a psychopathic personality.

However, after reaching a dead end road at a certain point in his life, he found himself alone in his prison cell, face-to-face with the sudden manifestation of a spiritual phenomenon, which miraculously initiated a positive transformation in his life.

It was the impetus that provided needed strength to the weak to overcome long-held vices; and which fostered confidence in one who had low self-esteem, enabling him to believe that success is attainable. Thus, a divine mission was given to a life that lacked purpose.

This book is a practical guide for educators, therapists, counselors, criminal justice instructors, and facilitators of life skills and cognitive self-change programs. This practical guide is a source of help for individuals and groups struggling with deviancy issues such as low self-esteem, illiteracy, thug life, alcoholism, drug addictions, crime, correctional institutionalization, and lack of personal accountability.

Contents

ACKNOWLEDGEMENTS

In the text of the book, I have mentioned by name a number of wonderful people who were influential in my life, and have helped to set my life on the right course. I want to thank all of these people and I am truly humbled and grateful for all the generous opportunities, privileges, and blessings that have been bestowed upon me since I set my life in a new direction. All those listed below deserve and will receive my generous thanks.

Mr. Richard and Mrs. Betty Tinnin, my late parents who provided me and my twelve siblings with all the basic provisions and life skills a child would need to survive and excel in life if one so chose.

The Rest of My Family, which includes my siblings, aunts, uncles, in-laws, nieces, nephews, and cousins, for supporting me whenever I was in the right and for loving me whether I was right, wrong or indifferent.

My Dear Children, for all the years I missed being in their lives as a result of my repeated trips to jail and prison but yet maintained their allegiance with me and visited me more than I deserved. I extend a special thanks and appreciation to my biological son Mr. Robert Pinkton and to my six biological daughters Mrs. Tawona Gee, Miss Stephanie Tinnin, Miss Cassandra Tinnin, Ms. Joycelyn Johnson, Mrs. Nicole Hutchison, and Miss Kelly Walton. I also extend a special thanks and appreciation to my three step-daughters Karri Young, Keonna Young, and Chanell Whitney for enduring twelve years of my brand of fatherhood.

Ms. Kathy Price, who I just met this past May 2009 at our family's Memorial Day celebration in Fort Wayne, Indiana. She demonstrated at that time unyielding encouragements and powerful influences that I should immediately write this book as a result of a discussion we had just shared concerning my passion to uplift others through the presentation "Cycle / Psycho Personality" and through other public venues.

Mr. Stephen Guy, my former English professor, who recently retired from Ball State University, and who, along with his beautiful wife Cynthia, had become a dear and personal friend about eight years ago and had always encouraged me to write a book and that he would edit the book free of charge. I immediately requested him to edit my book once I completed it and he instantly obliged.

Mr. Mark Coonan, a former fellow prisoner and dear friend for over 20 years, for his encouraging words that influenced me to enroll in a college program while incarcerated at the Indiana State Reformatory (currently the Pendleton Correctional Facility) and for his assistance in the enrollment process. He also assisted Stephen Guy in some measure in the editing of my book.

Mr. Rodney "Rod" Ross, a dear friend, confidant, and former co-worker when I was employed at Meridian Transition School and who is a prolific artist that provided his artistic skills to the graphics on the cover of this book. If you are anyone you know has an interest in Mr. Ross' graphic design services then he can be reached through his e-mail rossconcepts@aim.com.

Ms. E. Lois Thomas, who is my elder sister and one year my senior and who covered my backside throughout life, supported me endlessly during my 15 ½ years of incarceration, and assisted in a significant way in the acquisition of meaningful employment for me.

Mr. William G. Mays, President and CEO of Mays Chemical Company, along with his late brother Ted Mays, provided me with my first place of employment shortly after my release from prison. Mr. William G. Mays also established flexibility in my employment with his company whereas he allowed me to visit schools and other community organizations to perform motivational presentations during normal work hours as long as I made up the hours at work during late weekday evenings or on the weekends.

Mr. Theodore "Ted" Mays, former Vice-President of Mays Chemical Company and the late brother of William G. Mays, in addition to having an instrumental role in providing the first employment for me, he also was kind enough to give me a reliable car as a gift so that I could have independent transportation to work every day.

Mr. Bill West, Vice-President of Mays Chemical Company, for being such a dear friend, confidant, and always willing to contribute moral and/or material support in a righteous cause I may confront.

Mr. Olgen Williams, former Executive Director of the Christamore House and Family Center and currently the Deputy Mayor of Neighborhoods for the City of Indianapolis, for offering and providing me meaningful employment at the Christamore House in 2007 at a crucial time in my life and for becoming a genuine friend despite previous concerns.

Dr. Eugene White, Superintendent of Indianapolis Public Schools, for going way out on a limb where most high-profile personalities would not dare go to provide employment opportunities to a person with a criminal history. I thank Almighty God-Allah for your boldness, confidence, and generosity.

Dr. Vernon G. Smith, Indiana State Representative, for allowing me prior to my release from prison to be featured in one of his "scare straight" videos designed for a youthful audience to discourage deviant behaviors and encourage academic achievements. Also, for appointing me in 1995 to serve on the Planning Committee of the Indiana Commission on the Social Status of Black Males which exposed me to many prominent politicians and celebrities, and for being such a good friend and supporter since my release from prison 15 years ago.

Mr. Melvin "Mel" Greene, my former supervisor and former Director of Transition Programs of the Indiana Department of Correction. He became one of my very best friends and "brother in the struggle" to change the counter-productive thinking of incarcerated souls and to influence other young minds, that higher education, spiritual enlightenment, and a solid moral foundation are essential keys to a holistic development. My friend Mel is responsible for stirring me in a relationship with the Indiana Department of Correction in the year 2000. This relationship continues today, and it has consequently provided me with a wealth of experiences, which have contributed to my ability to influence positive behavior among many who struggle with deviant issues.

Mr. Robert "Bob" Ohlemiller, former Deputy Commissioner of the Indiana Department of Correction and current Program Director of the Marion County Jail, for his part in providing me a contractual employment opportunity in the year 2000 with IDOC which in turn created a security clearance for my person and enhanced my credibility as a citizen. Despite my termination from IDOC in 2004, Mr. Ohlemiller and I maintained a cordial friendship, met periodically for lunch with occasional employment prospects on the agenda, and recently discussed the prospect of me providing volunteer services at the Marion County Jail.

Mrs. Lilly Cosby, a very dear friend, confidant, and former Transition Coordinator at a Indiana Department of Correction facility and current Program Secretary at the Marion County Jail, for her unyielding support and assistance in my efforts to provide effective motivational presentations to offenders and for her insights and wisdom in other personal matters.

Mr. Damon Ellison, my former employer and the former Superintendent of the Marion County Juvenile Detention Center, for being immensely empathetic and incredibly concerned about the welfare of the youth detained under his watch and for being bold enough to hire men and women like myself that most youthful offenders respected and embraced the mentoring provided.

Ms. Saderia "Niambi" Means, my late and dear friend who mentored me in my public speech aspirations shortly after my release from prison and who introduced me into many Indianapolis Public Schools in 1995, and after, where I was provided opportunities to present motivational speeches to the student body and ultimately provided my current place of employment.

Mr. Otis "Big O" Brown, past owner of Nu Doo Barber Shop, my late and dear little "brother in the street struggle" to save our youth in the neighborhood of North Clifton Street who lost his life at the hands of those he tried to save. He and I spring-board off each other with positive affirmations daily while we were in prison and also during the many years of freedom while he operated his triad of legitimate businesses. We who loved him truly miss him and the neighborhood has suffered somewhat.

Brother R. Jones-Bey, National Grand Sheik of the Moorish Science Temple of America, for being incredibly supportive and allowing me and my volunteer missionary associates to continue our volunteer work inside Indiana prisons.

Brother R. Love El, former National Grand Sheik of the Moorish Science Temple of America, for introducing me into the volunteer system for Indiana prisons. Also, for inviting me to Temple #71 of the Moorish Science Temple of America in Washington, D.C. to receive direct instructions on the procedures of Friday Worship Services and Sunday School Services. In addition, for allowing me on many occasions to travel with him and his assistant Brother R. McDowell-Bey to various Indiana prisons; and for continually instructing and advising me via in person, on the phone, or in the mail about the Holy teachings of our illustrious and divine Prophet Noble Drew Ali.

Brother R. McDowell-Bey, Minister of Institutional Branch Temples in Virginia and Washington, D.C. for the Moorish Science Temple of America, for hosting me without expense in his home for five days in Washington, D.C. and for continually supporting, advising, and instructing me for the past 10 years on the Holy teachings of our illustrious and divine Prophet Noble Drew Ali.

Brother Lawrence Gregory-Bey, my dear and late Moorish brother, for over thirty years. He along with Brother Wilbur Moore-Bey, was one of my

Moorish kin who originated the idea, also, Brother R. Love El, recommended to the Department of Correction officials that I was the choice of the Moors incarcerated in Indiana prisons to function as their volunteer representative for Institutional Branch Temples of the Moorish Science Temple of America. While it is impossible to ascertain the exact number of brothers and sisters Brother L. Gregory-Bey taught and initiated into the Moorish Science Temple over the past 40 years, it is nonetheless estimated that this honorable Brother Gregory-Bey breathed that Holy Breath (Divine Truth) on innumerable pupils including myself. My dear Brother L. Gregory-Bey unjustly suffered the past 24 years of incarceration for a violent crime that DNA exonerated him on. However, the American court system refused to honor and that he ultimately suffered an unjustly and untimely demise in his prison cell just recently (October 17, 2009) and returned to the spirit plane to be with our FATHER GOD-ALLAH. The extensive profound wisdom and vast array of knowledge of Moorish Science that our dear Brother L. Gregory-Bey possessed will be sorely missed.

Brother Leroy Graves-El, my best friend and Moorish brother for over twenty years and whom I travel with to the various Indiana prisons to perform volunteer missionary services for the Moorish Science Temple of America.

Sister Andrea Leadford-Bey, is an excellent friend, and my Moorish sister, who proclaimed her nationality on January 15, 2009, (Moorish New Year). We travel to the various Indiana prisons to perform volunteer missionary services for the Moorish Science Temple of America.

Brother Achebe "Ralph" Turner, my dear friend for over forty years and my Islamic brother, teacher, and comrade "on the front line struggle" of liberation and justice for all worthy ex-offenders striving to have their convictions expunged and securing meaningful employment.

Mr. Clete Ladd, Principal of Indianapolis Metropolitan High School, my dear friend and brother on the "front line struggle" to teach and guide particularly our at risk youth in the direction of academic achievement and moral accountability. Brother Clete Ladd has never missed an opportunity in the past fourteen years to invite me to speak to his students or for him to accompany me to a prison to address offenders with his wide range of knowledge and wisdom.

Mr. Danny Graham, owner of Graham's Auto Repair, my dear friend and "silent brother in the street struggle" to provide employment opportunities for primarily ex-offenders and those disenfranchised souls who possess some reasonable auto mechanic skills and who desire to perform an honest day's work. In addition to taking good care of my vehicle, Danny's business provides a safe and neutral place for many of our old school friends to meet, greet, and congregate with one another. Danny has been very supportive in any righteous cause I undertook and has repaired my vehicle on many occasions and returned it to me without expense until I was able.

Mr. Donnie and Mrs. Minnie Dancy, for their unselfish support, contributions, and employment opportunities they provide to me and to a significant number of other individuals around the city of Indianapolis. I would be remiss if I failed to acknowledge the work I did delivering pizzas for D&C Pizza, humble work that I am privileged to do during the summer break when I am not working for the school system. My philanthropist friends Donnie and Minnie Dancy, who are happily married, own several D&C Pizza parlors around the city of Indianapolis. Though I am not part of their regular employee team, Donnie and Minnie allow me to work a few hours occasionally during the summer months to earn gas money for my automobile since the school system's budget during these critical economic times has no way for me to earn income during that period.

FINALLY, I cannot possibly thank my array of friends and family members each in an essay format but I can extend honorary mention to some like:

Jo Ann Hunter
Richard "Dickie" Tinnin
Phillip "Buck" Tinnin
Jacquelyn "Jackie" Kenton
Curtis "C.T." Tinnin, Sr.
Patricia "Pat" Cornell
E. Lois Thomas
Kermit "Ki Ki" Tinnin
Lucy Beth Tinnin
Lynn Irene Tinnin-Rowen
Charles "Chuck" Tinnin
Rhea Anthony "Tony" Tinnin
Misty Redmond
Tamika Gadis
Lee "June" Gadis, Jr.
Diane Hull
Denise Pruitt
Linda Shaw
Lori Hannah
Joyce Elaine Parker
Carla Patterson
Sylvia Marie Garcia Tinnin-Bey
Angelique Torrentino
Sherry Pinkton
Diane Maxie
Karen Marie Grundy-Hobbs
Dorothy Yvonne "Dotty" Hall
Regina Walton-Phillips
Samuel "Legs" Burton
Marcia Wilson
Stephanie Gardner
Holly Emery
Officer Donnie Allen
Trasheen Britt
Pauline Reeves
Jerri Pollard
Carmen Rivera
Sandra Robertson
Barbara Epps

Kay Toliver
Gerald "Jerry" Toliver
Robin Toliver
Kermit "Kakes" Tinnin
Batina "Tina" Tinnin
Corey "C-Town" Tinnin
Lynette Thomas-Foreman
Erica Thomas
Curtis Tinnin, Jr.
Retha Cornell-Swain
Joseph "Sean" Cornell
Jeffery "Jeff" Kenton
Cynthia Kenton-Jennings
Delores "Dee Dee" Redmond
Antton "Sugar Bugger" Gadis
Liflo Queary
Bridget Queary
Ona "Dee Dee" Hollins
Charissa Barnes
Valerie Parker
Steve Patterson
Marque Torrentino
Mikea Torrentino
William "B J" Rowen
Ricco Rowen
Ken Rowen
Sam Ricketts
Gwendolyn Nickson
David King
Kris Walker-Guess
Satishkumar Patel
Carlette Duffy
Otis "Little O" Brown Jr.
Kenny Caudle
Greg Johnson
Diane Petty
Cathy Williams
Yvonne Reeves
Joyce Warren

Robert Earl Badell
Robert Lewis McFarland
Brother Maurice May-Bey
Brother Michael "Goldie" Collier-Bey
Brother Ronald "Ronnie" Mason-Bey
Brother Rodney Williams-Bey
Brother Sylvester Moore-El
Brother Clifford Wilburn-El
Brother Frank James-Bey
Brother John Lane-El
Brother Mustafa Haneef-El (E. Ford-El)
Shelida Kerr
Karla Bibbs
Anthony "Danny Boy" Burris
Michelle Cannon
Jesse "LT" McElwain
Mary Kay McElwain-Tinnin-Phillips
Kevin "Peanut" Bluitt
Karen Vaughn
Sheri Williams
Dr. Omari Dyson
Dwayne "Wayne" Gee
Charles "Yirmeyahu" Burton
Tracy "Big Tracy" Vincent
Vonda Love
Andrenae "Pookie" Martin
Anita "Nita" Babb
Michelle "MeMe" Fields
Yvette Thompson
Evey Gaither
Christy Wadley
Kevin Garner
Darryl Hill
Craig Scott
Terri Tyree
Sarah Avant
Reverend Dave Rozzell
Jamie Rae Jenkins
Khabir Shareef
Wilbur "Face" Graham

Marshall "Shack" Shackleford
Donald "Eastside" Allen
Brother Steven Stanfield-El
Brother Danny Grundy-Bey
Brother Joseph Wilson-El
Brother Wilbur Moore-Bey
Brother Garland Jeffers-El
Brother Elihu Johnson-Bey
Brother Phillip McBrady-Bey
Brother Johnny Jones-Bey
Brother Clifford Jackson-Bey, Jr.
Kelvin Tyrone Brown
Dyirica "Rica" Bacon
Anthony "AO" Owens
Sherry Mooney
Irish "Sissy" Hampton-McElwain
Lois "Buddy" McElwain-Sullivan
Lisa "lisalovesthebeach" Edwards
Rev. Byron "Big Black" Vaughn
Maxine Bryant
Richard "Richie" Cooper
Lloyd "Lee" Fuentes
Paul A. "PJ" Moore
Victor "Big Vic" Hutchison
Robert Love
Roselyn "Kay" Holloway
Aniteria "Niteria" Fowler
George Fields
Lonnie Belmar
Kim Boyd
Reggie Townsend
Inga Garner
Farid Abdul Rahim
Charles Robinson
Diane Harvey
Michael Kelley
Deborah "Dee Dee" Batts
Joyce Ann Grundy Barrows
Robert "Fish" Grice
Ronald "Mook" Graham

Section I.

Imprisonment

On November 30, 1979, I was sentenced to two years imprisonment for possession of 1.9 grams of heroin. Since I was a habitual offender, that sentence was increased to thirty years.

By 1988, I had been incarcerated at the Indiana State Reformatory for nine years. Again, in the same year, I appeared before the Indiana Parole Board for a clemency hearing, with the hope of receiving a clemency release from prison at that time. Unfortunately, I was not even close to being eligible for clemency, due essentially to my extensive criminal history. But the board recommended that I seek drug abuse counseling while in prison.

The Parole Board openly acknowledged that my problems with criminal activity seemed directly related to my drug addiction. In response to the Board's recommendation, I immediately enrolled in the prison's drug rehabilitation program.

Shortly thereafter, the prison's substance abuse counselor sent a pass for me to meet with him at his office. Two primary questions he asked me really summed up the crux of the interview with him. First, he asked whether I was still using drugs while in prison. I truthfully replied "no" and went on to explain that I had refrained from the use of tobacco products since and the use of illegal drugs, since 1985, when I adopted a religion to help me stay grounded.

The counselor next asked me what I was doing to better myself while in prison. Again, I honestly informed him that I was taking college courses in the Ball State University program, majoring in speech communications, which included public speaking courses. In addition, I expressed my desire to become a public speaker some day.

At that point, the counselor apparently became impressed with my positive, self-imposed transformation and decided that I did not need his drug rehabilitation program. However, he informed me that a speaking opportunity was available for offenders to address teen students who were bused to the prison to participate in a "Scared Straight" program. He offered to submit my name as a speaker, with my permission. With subtle excitement brewing inside me, I instantly responded, "I would be delighted to speak to the teen students." That marked the beginning of my public speaking career.

1991 Herald-Bulletin Newspaper photo of S.A. seated while addressing youth in a Scare Straight Program at Pendleton C.F.

Various groups of teen students visited the Indiana State Reformatory every Monday and Wednesday to be, *so to speak*, "scared straight." There must have been something about my presentation, because, after a few years, I noticed that the other speakers were gradually eliminated from the program and only my services were utilized for the "Scared Straight" program.

With extreme passion and an intense desire to change the minds of those who were traveling down the path of self-destruction, I delivered conscience-searing messages in my presentations. But I did not realize just how much impact these presentations were having until the media began to show an interest.

The presentations were conducted in a section of the prison's administration building not accessible to the general prison population. It was the same room in which the Indiana Parole Board held its hearings.

On most occasions, I would have an audience of approximately 25 to 30 students, seated in rows at one end of the large room. At least three to four accompanying teachers, parents, or school officials would seat themselves amongst the students.

At the conclusion of the presentations, the visiting adults would approach me to identify themselves and comment on the presentation. They would tell me how they hoped certain students in attendance would heed the warnings and positive messages in my speeches.

On one particular occasion at the conclusion of my presentation, I was greeting several visitors who had accompanied a group of students to the prison. A relatively young European American (commonly called white) woman, whom I had assumed was a teacher, parent, or school official, approached me with her right hand extended. With a gracious smile, I gladly and politely shook her hand and to my surprise, she simultaneously identified herself as a representative of the Anderson, Indiana *Herald/Bulletin* newspaper. She asserted that my presentation was powerful and full of impact and it was her hope that the students would heed what they heard.

In my opinion, there was little difference between this presentation and the previous ones. They all related many of my unfortunate experiences resulting from bad decision-making, and the awful and sometimes very painful consequences, which followed.

1991 Herald-Bulletin, Newspaper photo of S.A. standing while addressing youth in a Scare Straight Program at Pendleton C.F.

Nevertheless, she requested permission from me to highlight my presentation and life story in her newspaper. I agreed and a couple weeks later (May 19, 1991), excerpts from my presentation and background information concerning various developments in my life were featured in a full-page story in the Lifestyle section of the Anderson, Indiana *Herald-Bulletin*.

That newspaper article became the talk of both inmates and staff at the prison facility. I enjoyed weeks of compliments and accolades, and I sent copies of the article to my family members in Indianapolis for them to read, hoping to generate some pride in a brother, a son, and a father who had disappointed and disgraced so many of his family members for too many years. In addition, I wanted my family to have the newspaper article laminated so my great-great grandchildren will someday read something positive that I did in my life for the benefit of others. This experience is what really gave me the motivation to believe that I could have a successful career in the public speaking arena at a suitable level of competency.

Once I was released from prison in 1994, I encountered a couple of friends, including biological brothers, Mark "Moe" Massey and Michael "Abdullah" Massey with whom I had been incarcerated at one facility or another, and they remembered my public speaking aspirations while in prison.

S.A. July 17, 1997 with Saderia Niambi Means in Circle Center Mall at Award Ceremony

These two brothers introduced me to the glorious and now late Ms. Saderia "Niambi" Means, who had been speaking to students in the Indianapolis Public Schools (IPS) system and in other venues around the Indianapolis area for years.

Niambi, as she was affectionately called, was the first person to introduce me as a motivational speaker to prominent personnel in the school system. This eventually opened the door to speaking engagements at a vast number of schools within the IPS district.

Over the next 10 years approximately, Niambi furnished me with tremendous insight and knowledge, which helped in making me an effective and successful personnel in the school system as well as a whole. To God and to this great and remarkable lady, I owe much for whatever successes I have achieved in community and social services and even in many aspects of my personal life.

Release

A little past midnight on December 9, 1994, forty-three year old Gregory Resnover was executed via the electric chair, at the Indiana State Prison. In my estimate, a substantial portion of the African-American community of Indianapolis believed and maybe continues to believe that Resnover was unjustly accused, tried, convicted, sentenced, and executed. Coincidentally, I was released from prison later that morning, after serving 15 ½ years.

Gregory and I were not accomplices in criminal cases, but we were accomplices in classroom antics as children growing up on the west side of Indianapolis, Indiana, and attending Indianapolis Public School #42. In fact, Gregory and I were both born in July 1951; I being only a few days his senior.

We attended the same grades throughout elementary school and shared the same homeroom during many semesters. We knew each other very well. A number of other students in our peer group exhibited counter-productive behaviors that qualified them as members of the class clowns, and which later directed their path to turbulent and sometimes violent futures.

Some class clowns in school #42 of the latter 1950s through the mid-1960s who undoubtedly had the makings of Oscar nominees were young men such as, Aaron Taylor, Anthony "Buddy" Ballard, Anthony "Danny Boy" Burris, Anthony "Tony" Folley, Anthony "A.O." Owens, Clay Byers, D'Coby McGuire, Frank "Johnny" Harris, Gregory "Gis"

Resnover, Jesse Lester, Jesse "LT" McElwain, John Foster, Keith Lewis, Larry King, Lonnie Belmar, Nathaniel "Nate" Allen, William "Butch" Mitchell, William "June Bug" Smith, Lawrence "Monk" Harris, the twins Ernest and Bernice McClain, and me, S. A. Tinnin-Bey (formerly Steven Tinnin).

Sadly, by the first one or two semesters of high school practically the entire unofficial membership of our class clown group had dropped out of school for a life in the streets. We were already travelling fast down a road of self-destruction, and once we dropped out of school our speed down that destructive road accelerated as we raced to the edge of total self-annihilation.

I hope you will understand and acknowledge a logical explanation later in this book, the use of the term *self-annihilation.* Whenever an individual makes a conscious decision to engage in behavior that could be potentially destructive in a physical, mental, and/or spiritual way, the destructive consequences, produced by bad decisions, are self-induced. And since the affected individual is the only person responsible for the bad behavior, he or she must suffer the consequences.

By the early 1960s, we were teenagers and strongly attracted to a number of cultural vices and gang-oriented associations that many rowdy, aggressive, and potentially violent teenage boys experience in "the hood," commonly known as low-income neighborhoods. By the latter part of that same period, I, in particular, and our group in general, made some very bad decisions that had long-lasting effects. Some of us lived long enough to regret them and subsequently amended the associated behavior. But others were not so fortunate and had their lives cut tragically short.

First Employment Opportunity

By January 20, 1995, approximately forty-two days after my release from prison, I acquired my first job with the assistance and influence of my older sister E. Lois Thomas. She at that time was a fifteen-year employee at Mays Chemical Company in Indianapolis.

Bill Mays, Pres. CEO of Mays Chem. Co. presents 5-yr. Employee Award to S.A. n 2000

In mid-January, around lunchtime, Lois telephoned and instructed me to get over to Mays Chemical Company right away so that she could introduce me to her employer, William G. Mays, president and C.E.O. of the company and one of the wealthiest and most accomplished African-American males in Indiana.

I was legally unable to drive myself there at that time, so I implored my eldest daughter Tawona to drive me to the Company for an impromptu interview with Mr. Mays. Prior to my meeting with Mr. Mays, I had been made aware that he is a multi-millionaire and that, in addition to the Mays Chemical headquarters in Indianapolis, he owns at least one Mays Chemical Company in Chicago, Illinois, and another in Taylor, Michigan.

I did not have to wait long. My sister Lois's official position in the company was assistant comptroller, and the moment the receptionist, Lisa, notified her of my arrival, she immediately came out of her office to meet me in the lobby. Lois greeted me with a big hug and a sisterly kiss and then directed me to follow her into Mr. Mays' office. Once I was inside the office, Mr. Mays greeted me with a genuine smile and generously extended his right hand. I instantly accommodated him with a humble extension of my own hand and was thrilled to be in the presence of such a man. But even with his towering community stature as a wealthy philanthropist, he exuded a "down-to-earth" persona. He is a very busy man, so we quickly turned our attention to my purpose for being in his office.

He immediately told me that he was aware of my recent release from prison and my need for a job. He also told me that he had learned about some of my academic, vocational, therapeutic, and civic achievements during my incarceration and asserted that he was impressed with them. My immediate gratitude led me to be open and honest about my past brushes with the law. I outlined my plan to give back to the community by giving motivational speeches that would discourage youth from pursuing a self-destructive path, which could result in jail time, premature death, or serious damages to the larger community.

In our discussion, Mr. Mays was genuinely objective and even empathetic concerning my unfortunate past. In addition, he was greatly impressed by my earnest attempt to make reconciliation with my community for my past misdeeds. It took no time for me to realize that Mr. Mays was a kind, generous and understanding man.

Obviously impressed with the results of our brief, yet productive meeting, Mr. Mays instructed Lois to introduce me to his brother Ted Mays and to have him determine the appropriate place for me to work in this company. At that time, Ted was one of the vice-presidents of the company and was just as warm and friendly as his brother.

Ted had me fill out an employment application and subsequently assigned me to the building maintenance department. This marked the beginning of a six-year stint with the prestigious Mays Chemical Company. I worked in the maintenance department until my resignation in January 2001. I was then offered simultaneous employment contracts with the Indianapolis Public Schools and the Indiana Department of Correction, which I accepted.

It would be remiss on my part if I fail to credit Mr. Mays for two other benefits I enjoyed as his employee. First, he allowed me to start my own evening janitorial cleaning service after five months of employment in his company, by contracting me to clean several other buildings he owns in Indianapolis. Secondly, he instructed the supervisor of the maintenance department, Craig Scott, to assign me to maintain the property at Mr. Mays's home in the Geist Reservoir area. I faithfully fulfilled both obligations with virtually no supervision, until my resignation in January 2001.

During my six-year employment at Mays Chemical Company, I was allowed to accept public speaking invitations from various middle and high schools, colleges, universities, juvenile and adult correctional facilities, drug and alcohol rehabilitation centers, and community and government organizations. There was never a problem leaving my job to fulfill those obligations, as long as my absence from work did not occur too frequently. Besides, many of my speaking engagements occurred after work hours or on the weekends. This lessened the problem of frequently missing hours of work and placing my employment at risk.

My regular speaking engagements throughout Indiana, and perhaps the effectiveness of those presentations, influenced both the Indiana Department of Correction and the Indianapolis Public Schools to offer me contractual employment opportunities during the mid and latter portions of 2000.

Section IV

Simultaneous New Job Opportunities

My first meeting with Indiana Department of Correction (DOC) officials occurred around the summer of 2000 and my first meeting with Indianapolis Public Schools (IPS) officials occurred around Christmas of that same year. Nevertheless, I signed contracts with both organizations on the same day in mid-January 2001. While my contract with IPS went into effect immediately, with the DOC it did not go into effect until February 1, 2001.

My IPS contract assigned me to New Beginnings High School, and its principal, Greg Allen. My job was to facilitate training in basic life skills in at least three classes of his students two mornings each week.

New Beginnings was an alternative high school for teenage youth with behavioral and/or attendance issues. Many of the students had been released from a detention facility and placed on probation or some kind of electronic monitoring. Mr. Allen gave me the freedom to accommodate the classes on the two mornings most convenient to my personal schedule.

This arrangement was perfect for me and officials of the Indiana Department of Correction allowed me similar liberty to schedule the times and days for providing professional services to initially ten adult correctional facilities. After reporting to the John Morton-Finney Building, the headquarters of the Indianapolis Public Schools, and signing the contract with IPS, I met with DOC officials later that same afternoon to sign a contract with them.

Back in the summer of 2000, I met with Indiana Department of Correction Commissioner Edward Cohen, Deputy Commissioner Robert J. Ohlemiller, and Director of Transition Programs Melvin Greene, for the first time. The purpose of our meeting was to discover exactly what professional services I could offer, and to determine whether I could actually meet the immediate needs of the DOC. The proposal made by these officials was incredibly challenging, but attainable. I was informed that the DOC had a crucial problem with overcrowding of its facilities and that the overcrowding was primarily the result of recidivism. I was further informed that the taxpayers of Indiana were opposed to funding any more prison construction. The DOC officials indicated to me that many strategies had already been implemented in an effort to reduce prison overcrowding but to no avail. For that reason, they inquired whether I could devise a presentation that could effectively discourage offenders from repeat offences.

While my knowledge of Principal Greg Allen prior to my meeting with him at the school was limited, I knew he had previously been vice-principal at Arlington High School in Indianapolis and the husband of a former Mays Chemical Company employee. However, I knew a little more about two of the DOC officials with whom I was about to meet. Commissioner Edward Cohen, the highest-ranking official of the Indiana Department of Correction, had been the warden at the Indiana State Prison and I believe, the superintendent at two other Indiana prisons while I was incarcerated in the Indiana prison system. However, I was not familiar with Deputy Commissioner Robert J. Ohlemiller until his introduction at this first meeting. Mr. Ohlemiller and I however developed a tremendous amount of respect for each other and a cordial working relationship during my three-year contract with DOC.

After my termination from DOC, Bob Ohlemiller and I would occasionally encounter each other at various public events. Soon we began meeting for lunch. We met at different times to discuss matters surrounding his new job with the Marion County Sheriff's Department and matters surrounding my new employment at given times, or my unemployment, depending on the situation at a particular time in my life. As a result of these meetings, Bob Ohlemiller and I eventually became great friends. At the same time, my friendship with Melvin Greene, Director of Transitions Programs, blossomed.

I was already familiar with Mel prior to my contract with DOC because he and I were members of the Indiana Commission on the Social Status of Black Males at that time. While working on that commission, we often enjoyed personal encounters with each other as speakers and subsequently became friends. I suspect that he is responsible for initiating and fostering the idea among DOC heads that I could provide a potential cure to some of the Department's problems with prison overcrowding. I also imagine that he conjured the idea that I could possibly provide such a solution based not only on his many experiences in the audience and on the periphery observing my public speeches, but also on our many in-depth, personal conversations on a multitude of topics.

The premise of the meeting was partially based on whether I could address offenders in transition/pre-release/re-entry programs at the various (initially ten) correctional facilities and produce a presentation designed to discourage offenders from repeated crimes. The meeting with all three officials of the DOC was convened downtown on the third floor of the Indiana Government Center South, the Central Office of the Department of Correction. I was warmly greeted by all in attendance and they immediately addressed the purpose for my invitation to the meeting.

Commissioner Ed Cohen began by stating that DOC officials had been monitoring my public speaking activities in the community as well as activities in my personal life. He indicated that they were hearing many good things about me and that they were impressed with the positive influences I was having on individuals and programs. He went on to ask if I would be interested in going back into the prisons to give motivational presentations to offenders in transition programs and provide volunteer representation for the Moorish Science Temple of America, an Islamic organization whose members practice the religion of "Islamism." I replied that I was interested first, because I love public speaking and second, I would welcome the opportunity to represent the Islamic organization of which I had been a member since 1985. Obviously pleased with my response, Mr. Cohen added that I would work under contract and that I would receive monetary compensation for the transition program portion of the contract only. He further explained that the government cannot legally provide monetary compensation for religious services.

Shortly thereafter, however, a third segment of the proposed contract was added when DOC officials recommended that I participate in a 40-hour cognitive self-change training program titled "Thinking for a Change," which was scheduled for August 2000. This program incorporates three basic life skills: thinking, social, and problem-solving skills, in a 22-lesson format. I participated in the program and achieved national certification as well as monetary compensation for its facilitation in the prison system.

I had agreed to provide DOC with three types of professional services; however, I would be paid for only two of the professional services, the Transition programs and the Thinking for a Change program. In addition to the three professional services offered, I was also volunteering time to the Moorish Science Temple of America programs, which involved traveling, at my own expense, to ten correctional facilities. Within six months of the execution of my original contract with DOC, eight additional facilities, six adult and two juvenile, would be added to the list of institutions. These I visited every fourteen days on schedule. Out of those eighteen facilities, two were juvenile, four were adult female, and twelve were adult male.

Prior to the conclusion of the meeting by the DOC officials, for that afternoon, Mr. Cohen directed my attention to a huge white three-ring notebook that he retrieved from another location nearby. It appeared to be about one half foot in thickness and on the front cover were two names of a single person typed in big, bold letters, one above the other. I instantly recognized both names as my former and current names. My former name, Steven Alexander Tinnin, was the one above and my current name, Saddam Ali Tinnin-Bey (a.k.a. Brother S. A. Tinnin-Bey), was the one below. Mr. Cohen then randomly opened the notebook to expose some of its contents to me. He then looked directly into my eyes, as I gazed into his. With sheer confidence he stated, "We know everything about you and we believe you are who you say you are," as if to give me the impression that the DOC had assigned undercover investigators to conduct surveillance on me for an extended period of time, and subsequently reported their findings to the DOC. That really did not disturb me as much as most people might think. I reasoned that the DOC has a security interest in having a substantial amount of intelligence in advance, on anyone who is to be allowed entry into a correctional facility. Such concerns, I realized, would be especially serious concerning someone formerly incarcerated.

Actually, DOC officials had initiated my speaking career in the prison system under an underwritten pilot agreement during the summer of 2000 right after my very first meeting with department heads. Melvin Greene, the director of transition programs, was initially assigned to drive me to a few of the correctional facilities over the next couple of months and familiarize me with the pertinent administrators and staff at the various institutions on whom I would be relying to assist me in my work in those facilities. Apparently, Mr. Greene was also to use these occasions to observe me as I addressed the offenders in transition programs and measure the impact the presentations had on them. My presentations were primarily about my personal background: my lack of education while growing up, my gang involvement, my abuse of drugs, and my run-ins with the law. Most importantly, what I had to say about how I overcame my deviant behaviors and became a model citizen.

Of course, the staff at the various correctional facilities did not always see me as that model citizen. My introduction into the prison system as a former offender and now as a professional citizen was not always well received by correctional staff and administrators. On one of the first occasions during the pilot program when Mr. Greene and I were visiting various facilities on behalf of the Commissioner's office, we were initially refused admittance into the Correctional Industrial Facility in Pendleton, Indiana, by the superintendent of that facility, supposedly because of my status as an ex-offender. By that time (summer 2000), I had been out of prison almost six years and had not encountered any problems with the law since. However, I was not surprised by the opposition we encountered at that particular facility. During my 15½ years of incarceration, I was transferred there from another facility and then to a third facility within 60 days for doing exactly what DOC was about to pay me to do, i.e., promoting peace, encouraging righteousness and literacy, and raising the consciousness of the prison population.

Nevertheless, though I was fairly calm about the rejection, Mr. Greene was disappointed and visibly upset about the superintendent's decision. Mr. Greene suddenly and hastily headed for the exit doors, and I quickly followed behind him to return to the parking lot and the state vehicle we had driven. Once Mel Greene got to the vehicle, he retrieved his mobile phone and dialed the Commissioner's telephone number to report the situation we had encountered and the superintendent's refusal to allow me inside the facility.

I did not attempt to listen to the verbal exchange between Mel and Commissioner Ed Cohen, and therefore, I cannot testify concerning the content of the conversation between the two. However, Mel later unfolded to me their conversation, which included the Commissioner's promise to phone that superintendent immediately to instruct him "to allow Mel and I into that facility if he cherished his job." It worked! Within minutes, Mel and I were entering the facility to conduct the business we had been sent to perform.

Over the next 12 months or so, limited opposition to my professional services occurred at a few institutions. Nevertheless, those oppositions fizzled out very quickly once the antagonists suspected intervention from facility administrators or Central Office.

On February 1, 2001, the pilot program for me ended and the actual contract employment with DOC began. I started with ten facilities: the Indiana State Prison, the Correctional Industrial Facility, the Lakeside, Westville, Wabash Valley, Branchville, Miami, Pendleton, Plainfield, and Putnamville Correctional Facilities. These constitute the ten major correctional facilities in Indiana. Once every fourteen days I was required to visit these facilities and provide professional services.

The Indiana State Prison, Wabash Valley, and Westville Correctional Facilities all have super maximum-security lockup units within their facilities. My professional services extended to visiting these units on occasions as long as I maintained my chaplaincy thus my status as the representative for the Moorish Science Temple of America. My primary duties were to provide motivational presentations to the transition/re-entry program, facilitate a cognitive self-change (Thinking for a Change) program, and volunteer representation for a religious group (Moorish Science Temple of America) within DOC facilities.

Contrary to the belief of many, some inmates opposed my coming into the prisons, at least to represent the Moorish

Bro. R. Love El, Natl. G.S. 1998 visit Moors at Wabash Valley C.F.

Science Temple of America (M.S.T. of A.) In the first few weeks of visiting my assigned facilities, I discovered that a couple of facilities in northern Indiana have a M.S.T. of A. program. The majority of their memberships do not believe that Prophet Noble Drew Ali founded the brand of Moorish Science Temple of America under the leadership of National Grand Sheik Brother R. Love El. And since my membership in the organization is consistent with the leadership of Brother R. Love El, then the northern sect began to view me as an adversary. The Indiana inmates who claimed membership in the "other" purported M.S.T.A. group appeared to be in the minority when considering Indiana prisons as a whole. Much of the opposition to my religious representation stemmed from offender members of the M.S.T.A. program housed at the State Prison in Michigan City, Indiana. Due to concerns for my personal security and the integrity of the program, I eventually abstained later in 2001 from returning to that facility. However, things apparently did not work out favorably in the long run for that M.S.T.A. program at the Indiana State Prison because some 8 years later the chaplaincy there would make a request on behalf of the offenders for me to resume representation there.

By February 2004, my contract services expired with DOC. I then returned to Ball State University during summer school of that same year to complete my Associate's Degree in communications.

After four years hiatus from IDOC involvement, in 2008 Reverend Dr. Stephen Hall, Director of Religious Services and Community Involvement for the Indiana Department of Correction, contacted me by phone. He inquired about my level of interest in returning to the prison system to provide volunteer representation for Moorish Science Temple of America programs, at least at a few correctional facilities in close proximity with my hometown of Indianapolis. I accepted and began providing these new rounds of volunteer services accompanied by several other volunteer Moorish associates. Services were provided only on weekends since our volunteer associates worked regular jobs during the weekdays.

By June 2009, our volunteer Moorish group consisted of Brother Leroy Graves-El, Sister Andrea Leadford-Bey and me. At this same time, we had acquired our 8th facility, which we agreed to provide volunteer services, the Indiana State Prison. The offender membership of M.S.T.A. at this facility in 2001 was predominantly hostile to me being a part of the representation for this community but now seem very receptive.

We met with the M.S.T.A. offender leadership and agreed that our volunteer Moorish group would function as civilian representatives and advisors for the offender's M.S.T.A. program at that facility.

<hr>

Section V

Decline of Indiana's Prison Population

According to IDOC Chief Communications Officer Douglas S. Garrison, in a report published on March 18, 2009:

"The Indiana Department of Correction (IDOC) has been studying and monitoring Indiana's recidivism rates for the past four years. Now, researchers have found that the overall recidivism rate has declined for the third consecutive year to 37.4%.

The IDOC defines recidivism as an offender's return to incarceration within 3 years of his release date from a state correctional institution. An offender is included in this study when they are released via one of the following avenues: Community Transition Program (CTP), Probation, Parole, or Discharge. Once released, an offender is verified as a recidivist if they return to the institutional custody of the IDOC for a new conviction or a technical violation of post-incarceration supervision.

For offenders released in 2005, only 37.4% have returned to prison by 2008, which is lower than the 2007 recidivism rate of 37.8%. Rates for 2005 and 2006 were 39.2% and 38.6%, respectively. During those four years, the demographics of the offenders studied remained consistent.

In addition, one statistic regarding a class of offenders shows a great deal of promise. The recidivism rate for sex offenders returning on a new sex offense was 1.05%, one of the lowest in the nation. In a time when sex offenders continue to face additional post-release requirements that often result in their return to prison for violating technical rules such as registration and residency restrictions, the instances of sex offenders returning to prison due to commitment of a new sex crime is extremely low.

These improving recidivism numbers demonstrate that the IDOC's focus on the successful re-entry of offenders in recent years is beginning to pay off. Indeed, all IDOC staff members across the state have worked hard to prepare offenders for their release back into their communities and give them the tools to succeed.

Even though conventional wisdom would have us believe recidivism is inevitable, I firmly believe that the hard work and dedication of IDOC staff has proven that the successful re-entry of offenders is more than possible," commented IDOC Commissioner Edwin G. Buss, who recently was appointed to the Office of the Commissioner. "The third consecutive decline in Indiana's recidivism rate is good for all, offenders, IDOC staff members, and Indiana taxpayers alike."

The IDOC's Research and Planning Division collected, analyzed, and presented the recidivism data.

Now, I am not sure whether the aforementioned DOC officials attributed any of the decline of the recidivism rate in Indiana to the motivational presentations I gave for DOC's re-entry programs from 2001 through 2004, but, if not, I will just have to usurp a little of the credit here. Though I performed a few other presentations and facilitated basic life skills classes for DOC, I am very confident that the presentation "CYCLE / PSYCHO" has been exceptionally effective.

To this day, countless former inmates and former participants in other social programs who listened to my speech in the past have approached me and made positive comments about that particular presentation. In fact, "CYCLE / PSYCHO" is the only presentation that the Fathers and Family Resource/Research Center has required me to perform for its program for the past 8 years. So this is evidence that some folk other than I, think highly of the "CYCLE / PSYCHO" presentation.

Section VI

Fathers and Family Resource/Research Center

The Fathers and Family program serves young men between 16 and 28. It helps fathers, or those who are about to become fathers and are struggling with the responsibilities of fatherhood. These young men attend classes and are given instructions that equip them with the tools and skills to become employable providers for their families. It also provides positive role models for their children; leaders in their families and communities, and overall great fathers. The established curriculum for this program is carried out over a six-week period. I am called upon to speak to practically each new class. Sometime in 1995, an employee of the Fathers and Family program, Brother Khabir Shareef, was the first to provide me an opportunity to address the young male participants in that program. Since then the Director Dr. Wallace McLaughlin and Coordinator Diane Bohannon of that program are generally the two persons responsible for securing my professional services at least three to four times each year.

Return to College

In order to fulfill my present obligations, I continually aspire toward the improvement of my educational standard and the subsequent development of a more credible status. Having completed a number of courses at Ball State University during my incarceration (1979-1994) at the Indiana State Reformatory (now the Pendleton Correction Facility), I needed only two more classes to earn my Associate of Arts degree.   For five consecutive weeks, Monday through Friday, I commuted between Indianapolis and Muncie, Indiana to attend these classes.

In the meantime, I was able to survive financially and spiritually because of the love, caring, understanding, and benevolence of my queen (fiancée), Joyce Elaine Parker. She and I shared a home, and she paid all the bills and provided the food while I was unemployed and traveling from Indianapolis to summer school on the campus of Ball State University in Muncie.   Joyce, who I affectionately call Lil' Mama, also provided food and shelter for her three young daughters (my step-daughters) who lived with us. It surely did not hurt to have such a wonderful woman like Lil' Mama in my life at such a crucial time. I do not think many women would have been so considerate to support a man in that situation especially with a total of five mouths to feed and the other responsibilities that arise in a household of five people. So I extend special honors and gratitude to this giant of a lady.

I would have loved to continue my higher education at that time to earn a Bachelor of Arts degree, but financial hardship for my family and I was too great to put schooling ahead of meaningful employment. Once I acquired the diploma for my associate's degree after five weeks of summer school, I immediately secured employment in Indianapolis with the Marion County Juvenile Detention Center.

Employment with Juvenile Detention Center

It may have helped that I was already familiar with Damon Ellison, the Superintendent of the Marion County Juvenile Detention Center, at the time I applied for employment in 2004. In fact, he and his family have been friends of my family since the 1950s or early 1960s. Mr. Ellison is around the age of my older sisters Lois and Pat and attended Shortridge High School with them. At one point, I was led to believe he was a little "fresh" on Lois at one time. Anyway, it turned out that he knew more about my background and criminal history than I knew about him. He was also aware that I had, within the last 10 years, turned my life around and had developed a reputation throughout the community as an outstanding leader and motivational speaker on youth, and adult issues.

Because of his many contacts in the criminal justice field, Mr. Ellison was aware of the good work I had done under contract with the Indiana Department of Correction. I take this opportunity to honor and commend this great man for all the genuine care and concern he provided for the youth who were detained in the Marion County Juvenile Detention Center. I deeply appreciate the chance he has given me to build my credibility by allowing me to work with the youth at that center, despite my extensive criminal history.

I worked at the Juvenile Detention Center from September 2004 until October 2006. My entry-level position was youth manager but amazingly, within those two years, I was rewarded twice with major promotions. It was probably because of my lengthy corrections background that I quickly adapted to this security-oriented job and achieved credibility.

In November 2005, about fourteen months into my employment at the detention center, I was promoted to assistant shift supervisor. Nine months later, in August 2006, I was promoted to shift supervisor in partnership with my shift supervisor Joyce Warren. We were both responsible for the operation and security of the entire facility during our eight-hour shift unless, other higher-level administrators were on site during that shift.

Although I was forthright about my criminal history during the employment application process and listed my three felony convictions on the face of the employment application, controversy about my extensive criminal history arose after the departure of Superintendent Damon Ellison. The local media got involved in October 2006 and influenced new administrators at the detention center to fire me.

Section IX

Employment with the Christamore House

Six months later, in April 2007, Olgen Williams, Executive Director of the Christamore House Family and Community Center, contacted me by phone and offered me a position with his community organization. Like a great number of other Indianapolis citizens, he was aware that my employment at the Marion County Juvenile Detention Center had been terminated. It had been repeatedly publicized for a couple of days on local television news and had been published in the *Indianapolis Star* newspaper on the morning of October 21, 2006. I later discovered that the report had even been published on the internet. Nevertheless, Williams informed me

S.A. 2007 Graduating Job Readiness Training Class at Christamoore House

during our telephone conversation that he had heard Brother Achebe (Ralph) Turner mention my name on the "Amos Brown Show," a local daily radio program.

Brother Acebe, the radio guest on the show, is a longtime friend of mine and shares membership and leadership roles in M.O.V.E., Inc., a political organization of ex-offenders and other concerned citizens that advocate the expunging of convictions. At that time, Williams needed an available person, preferably an adult male, to take over a contractual job position in his organization that had been abandoned by a former contract employee. According to Williams, the mere mention of my name on the radio that day stimulated his memory of the controversy at the detention center and my unemployed status. He almost immediately decided to offer me that vacant position. So at the conclusion of the radio broadcast, Williams quickly contacted the radio station to speak with Brother Achebe to acquire my mobile phone number.

Mr. Williams opened our phone conversation by inquiring about my current employment situation and informing me that he had an open contractual position in his organization that he believed would be a perfect fit for me, if I were interested. He described the contractual position as "Re-integration Coordinator," a federally funded position designed to assist adult persons with re-integrating into their communities after being convicted, and in most cases, released from jail or prison for serious crimes. That definitely sounded like a position I would love to undertake because I had already developed a background in working successfully with the incarcerated as well as the formerly incarcerated. And, of course, I really needed a job because I would never be satisfied with merely receiving unemployment benefits. Without hesitation, I accepted Williams' job offer. I worked in that position for the next seven months, until the federal funding expired.

In advance of my employment at the Christamore House, I was made aware that the contractual position would last only through the end of the year (2007). I must mention here that prior to Mr. Williams' offer of employment; I was not just sitting around waiting for my next job to fall from the sky into my lap. I was on the internet every day filling out job applications on Monster.com, and on other occasions submitting written applications to former employers and to potentially new ones. I even attended political and social events and inquired of the many attendees, whether they knew of anybody hiring.

Section X

Second Employment Opportunity with IPS

On one fortunate occasion, I attended a combined gathering of law enforcement people, politicians, and clergy held in Indianapolis at the Eastside Baptist Church during the early months of 2007. The meeting, purportedly an amnesty program, was covered by the local media. It was designed to encourage people with outstanding criminal warrants, to voluntarily turn themselves in to authorities or to the clergy.

One of my six biological sisters, Patricia Cornell, a longtime member of Eastside Baptist Church, encouraged me to attend that meeting in hopes that she might introduce me to the Superintendent of Indianapolis Public Schools, Dr. Eugene White, or someone else there who might be in a position to provide me with or direct me to some meaningful employment. Pat's idea and encouragement worked for me; she was able to introduce me to Dr. White, who eventually hired me as a Behavior Adjustment Center Facilitator. Of course, I was honest with Dr. White as I had been with others regarding my criminal past. I even mentioned my unfortunate termination of employment at the detention center based on my criminal history, even though I had listed my felony convictions on the employment application.

Dr. White expressed his awareness of that situation, which made a lot of sense to me because the incident had been plastered all over the local television evening news.

Two months into my contractual employment (June 2007) with the Christamore House, Mark West, the Vice-Principal of Tech High School, telephoned me and told me that he had been instructed by his boss, Dr. Eugene White, to arrange a meeting with me to consider a job, working in an alternative high school. I met with Mr. West at Tech High School and accepted the offer to work as the Behavior Adjustment Center Facilitator (behavior specialist) at a newly opened facility, Meridian Transition School, where Mr. West would be promoted to principal. Like most so-called "alternative" schools, this one is comprised of students who have histories of behavioral and/or attendance issues.

I began work at Meridian Transition School in August 2007 while still working at the Christamore House. This necessitated an adjustment in my work schedule at the Christamore house in order to meet my obligatory morning and afternoon work schedule at the school. By December 2007, my contractual employment with the Christamore House had expired, and the school became my single place of employment.

Section XI

Appointment to Offender Re-entry Panel

Early in 2008, Olgen Williams was appointed to the Office of the Deputy Mayor of Neighborhoods by the newly elected Mayor of Indianapolis, Gregory Ballard. Shortly after being elected, Mayor Ballard created the Mayor's Office of Offender Re-entry Program and placed the Deputy Mayor of Neighborhoods in charge. Deputy Mayor Williams immediately appointed Sister Khadijah Muhammad as the Director of the

Offender Re-entry Program. Shortly thereafter Director Muhammad developed the Offender Re-entry Ex-Offender Panel. This consists of approximately ten ex-prisoners who have established themselves in the community as responsible citizens. These ex-prisoners would serve as advisees to the Mayor's Office on strategies that could make offender re-entry programs in Indianapolis more effective in meeting the needs of ex-offenders returning to their communities. Director Khadijah Muhammad selected me as one of her earliest appointees to the panel.

Section XII

Transfer to Francis W. Parker Montessori School

At this point, I wish to mention that during my tenure with the school system, I served at the Meridian Transition School for two years in the same capacity as a full-time employee, with full benefits. I was later transferred in May 2009 to Francis W. Parker Montessori School #56, which is also within the Indianapolis Public Schools District. The challenges at my new placement turned out to be far greater and the student population much larger than at my former school.

This Montessori school serves over 300 students as opposed to little over a hundred students at Meridian Transition. Whereas the grade levels at this Montessori school range from pre-school to 8th grade, at the Meridian Transition, the range is 7th to 12th grade.

It is a great pleasure and privilege to work with a much younger clientele and with some classes of students diagnosed as autistic—students who offer serious challenges. The administrators and staff at the former school (particularly

Principal Mark West, Vice-Principal Mrs. Kris Walker-Guess, Social Worker Ms. Stephanie Gardner, Secretary Ms. Diane Hunter, and School Police Officer Donnie Allen), were very polite to me. They made the work environment conducive to my success in influencing improvements in the behavior of many students. My current co-workers and administrators are equally accommodating and polite.

Section XIII

Book Based on Motivational Presentation

Now, I will more directly address the primary presentation "Cycle / Psycho Personality" that I performed in transition/re-entry programs at a number of DOC facilities for over 3 years. This presentation was also made available to community organizations, alcohol and drug rehabilitation centers, and various middle schools, high schools, colleges and universities. The information in this book is based on that very presentation.

DOC officials originally gave me the impression that they were primarily interested in my ability to produce some kind of therapeutic presentation that could effectively discourage offenders from habitual relapse. Obviously, I took DOC up on the challenge.

My contract with DOC specified that I provide my own transportation to and from the various correctional facilities in order that I may fulfill my contractual obligations. The drive to some of the facilities in cities outside of, but close to my hometown Indianapolis, took me only 45 minutes to an hour. Other facilities such as Miami Correctional and Wabash Valley

Correctional took approximately 1½ to 2 hours. However, drives to the Indiana State Prison and Branchville Correctional took at least three hours. Except on holidays and during extremely bad weather, I drove to facilities Mondays through Fridays consistently, for three years.

The bottom line is that I achieved a wealth of experience by sharing my presentation "Cycle / Psycho Personality" every day and sometimes twice a day, with a different group of offenders at facilities located in a common vicinity. I visited each facility every fourteen days to give the same presentation and on every occasion, my audience was comprised of a different group of offenders about to be released from prison within days or months. In addition, several of my professors who taught college classes in the prison system, invited me on campus after my release from prison, to give the "Cycle / Psycho Personality" presentation to their students as well, some of whom were honor students. I also had an abundance of other opportunities to make the very same presentation at several other venues, ranging from academic, therapeutic, and to community organizations.   The repeat performances of the presentation provided much practice as well as an opportunity to refine its content.

Oftentimes I was made aware that the presentation received decent reviews from those in attendance. Dr. Jerome Kotecki, who did not teach in the prison system but was my 2004 summer school health sciences instructor at Ball State University, invited me to do the presentation "Cycle / Psycho Personality" to the entire health department. My English instructor, Stephen Guy, and my speech communications instructors, Stephen Hartnett and Dr. Jon Rutter, who all taught in the prison system, provided me similar invitations.

On my release from prison, Stephen Guy provided me an opportunity to address honor students and faculty in the

English Department on the Ball State campus. Stephen Hartnett and Dr. Jon Rutter provided me several opportunities as well, to present the same information to national educational/political forums, twice in hotels in downtown Chicago and once on the campus of the University of Illinois at Urbana-Champaign.

I am now prepared to share the same information with the world because I am convinced that this presentation has been adequately tested and can now serve others effectively in book form; particularly those I am not able to reach in person.

Virtually every day over a three-year period, I repeatedly presented this information to thousands of offenders incarcerated in a number of Indiana correctional facilities as well as to some students and citizens located at a variety of places around Indiana and parts of Illinois. While I found presenting to the offender population rewarding, other venues I found just as rewarding included middle schools, high schools, colleges, and organizations that provide services to at-risk youth and to persons struggling with alcoholism and drug addiction. There was a period between 2001 through 2007 when these presentations occurred with significant frequency.

I consistently received warm and encouraging responses from offenders, correctional staff and administrators, coordinators of civilian programs, educators, and students who had been in the audience during one of my presentations. While I am out shopping, fueling up my car at a gasoline station, or attending a social event, I often encounter people who experienced one of my presentations. Many of these people have commented on the positive and negative aspects of the presentation, and the impact it has had on their lives.

I have personally enjoyed good reviews about this presentation over the past eight years and have especially enjoyed hearing about the positive effects it has had on others--

how they have followed its principles to overcome demons that previously imprisoned them.

It is my hope that the information in book form, will affect a wider audience who might be struggling with similar problems. Through this book, I hope to affect a deep-seated cure within individuals who have failed to receive the help purported by other remedies and solutions.

The structure of the presentation "Cycle / Psycho Personality" is built upon a circle of thinking and behavioral patterns. The central principle that the presentation sets out to establish is this: If a person is trapped in a c-y-c-l-e of negative and counter-productive thinking and behavior, then that person is apparently p-s-y-c-h-o (crazy). This approach may seem a bit harsh and at times condescending. Nevertheless, what should a doctor do when confronted with a patient whose illness will be difficult and painful to treat? That is a situation that demands the truth, however troubling.

Upon this premise, I present to the reader of this book the truth and nothing but the truth, so help me God!

~~~~~~~~~~

Chapter 1

Opening of the Presentation

My presentation usually begins with an introduction of the speaker. Once I am introduced to the audience by the host of the program, I immediately extend an enthusiastic greeting to all in attendance and repeat my name, "Brother S. A. Tinnin-Bey."

I then proceed to inform the audience that, in addition to giving speeches throughout Indiana for the past 14 years, I am currently a member of an Islamic organization identified as the Moorish Science Temple of America, Inc. and have been since 1985. After a brief discussion of my current fulltime employment with the Indianapolis Public Schools since August 2007, I then proceed to talk about my previous places of employment. These include; the Christamore House Family and Community Center from April to December 2007, the Marion County Juvenile Detention Center from 2004 to 2006, simultaneous contractual employment with the Indianapolis Public Schools, and the Indiana Department of Correction (IDOC) from 2001 to 2004. Finally, I mention my fulltime employment with Mays Chemical Company from 1995 to 2001.

To help substantiate and bolster my presentation, a map of Indiana is projected, via the overhead projector for the class to view. The map includes numbered markers that reflect the locations of ten major correctional facilities, interspersed throughout the state where my speeches were given. My audience is made aware that the presentation I am about to perform for them is the very same one I have performed throughout IDOC, and in other locations. This whole process is designed to establish my credibility and expertise, hoping that the audience will be convinced that I deserved to be heard.

My father Richard Alexander Tinnin's, November 2008 obituary.

After this introduction, I always begin my presentation by honoring my earthly father, Richard Alexander Tinnin, for producing and raising thirteen children. He took sufficient care of us all until we became grown (or until we defined ourselves as grown). He also secured additional employment to ensure family support; plus he abstained from activities that could jeopardize his ability to support his family. This initial statement is not intended to diminish the exceptional job my mother and grandparents did in their collaboration with our father to raise us. I singled out my father in the opening statement because my audiences are primarily men or young males. Since I am convinced that my father represented the epitome of a man, I believe it is important to all in attendance that I set the level of male expectations high. This is done early in the presentation in hopes of gaining the undivided attention of the serious and the not so serious listeners. I further explain to my audience that I extend great honors to my father because he was strong enough to resist the counter-productive temptations that many of us so easily succumb to.

My father had thirteen children. Times were tough economically from the 1940s to the 1960s but he resisted the temptation to commit crimes to provide for his family. Instead, he worked a second and even a third job to make ends meet rather than taking part in criminal activities. Pop, as I affectionately called my father, told me, "I cannot see myself in jail and unable to provide for my family." He also said that he could not see another man or a governmental system taking care of his thirteen responsibilities because then he, himself, "would not be a man."

As a young, uneducated and inexperienced boy, I did not appreciate what my father was trying to convey to me. Consequently, I failed to absorb that wisdom and continued down the road of life in a state of delusion and confusion. However, I eventually understood and appreciated much later, what my father tried to share with me.

The bottom line is that my father would work two or three jobs to provide for his family and for himself. He maintained his standard of what constitutes being a man, rather than placing himself in a situation where he would be unable to fulfill his obligations as a man. I knew that the information I was sharing with the audience about my father was affecting them internally, because of their facial expressions.

My extensive public speaking experiences have given me the ability to discern the meaning of many facial expressions and elements of body language. Many in the audience had children themselves. In most cases, they had no more than three children, and they felt guilty for not caring for them sufficiently. Thus, I could actually perceive the effects of the guilt and shame stirring inside their souls. This made me confident that I would gain their undivided attention, as their minds were now ripe for absorbing what I had to tell them. Of course, not every person in the audience was ready. A few individuals did not appear to be ready. I understood that some in the audience were there only because of an institutional policy, court order, or some other order. In such instances, these individuals would often display some resistance to instruction and motivation and were, in essence, a captive audience. This is where the next phase of the presentation becomes very important and effective, especially for hardcore members of the audience.

When a member of the audience is openly and insistently disruptive, I remind the audience that I have had members in previous audiences who had been convicted of murder, rape, robbery, child molestation, etc. and that there isn't much I have not already heard from members in an audience. I would then tell the disruptive person or persons that if they wished to leave they were free to do so. However, if they chose to remain in the audience, but continued to be disruptive, I would use my influence to have them escorted out of the program. They were informed that the information I had to offer to the majority, was too valuable to allow a few to deprive them (the majority) of its benefits. Maintaining a certain level of respect and complete control of the class is critical to creating an environment for teaching and learning.

After displaying the map of Indiana via overhead projector on a screen and discussing the many prisons I regularly visited around the state, I informed the audience about the title of the day's presentation, "CYCLE / PSYCHO."

Class participation in the delivery of the presentation is extremely important; hence, I usually solicit from the audience their assistance in teaching this class, by assuring them that they would be more apt to embrace and incorporate the day's lessons into their lives if they participated in the teaching. I then remind them that they had already spent days or perhaps weeks together in this class before I entered the room. Therefore, they already had an opportunity to become familiar with one another, and perhaps developed some level of trust; but they were meeting me for the first time and therefore did not have the opportunity to develop that same familiarity and trust. I would further explain that they would be more apt to trust and honor the lessons in this presentation coming from a class perspective instead of solely from me. This approach often proves effective in enhancing the success of the presentation.

Though I am not a certified medical doctor, I do believe I have been divinely inspired to prescribe medicine that can cure some common ills suffered by individuals in society. The medicines I prescribe are not pharmaceutical but are readily found within the recesses of the subconscious mind. The prescription for the cure is embedded within the presentation "CYCLE / PSYCHO." To benefit from its content, one has to be prepared to face his problem straightforwardly; just as a patient would, who has been given the tragic diagnosis of cancer or some other serious disease. Generally, a patient who has been diagnosed with an irreversible illness reacts with disbelief and subsequently denial. The patient may get a second, third, and even a fourth medical opinion. But once he or she is convinced that the diagnosis is accurate, the patient usually accepts the unfortunate news and moves to discover a remedy that could prolong survival.

Although shockingly offensive to some, I find it imperative to stun the conscience of the audience very early in the presentation with this statement: "I will prove with the preponderance of the evidence that each and every one of you is crazy. I will further prove that the words 'cycle' and 'psycho' are indeed related, in that if a person is trapped in a negative and counter-productive c-y-c-l-e of thinking and behaving, then that person is in fact p-s-y-c-h-o." In addition, to meet the agreement I originally entered into with the IDOC, I designed the presentation in a way that would cause members of the audience to recognize the insanity of some of their behaviors and consequently   make positive changes for themselves. I reasoned that for me to be successful, the presentation must function as a symbolic mirror that reflects things about us, that are defined by society as abnormal and deviant but which eludes our understanding. My hope is that ultimately, this method will effectively discourage people from repeating or initiating behaviors commonly deemed abnormal and deviant.

I announce the title of my presentation "CYCLE / PSYCHO" but never expose how the words appear in print until after I request the class to assist me in spelling the words. I would then approach the white dry-erase board with a dry-erase marker in my hand while simultaneously asking the class to help me spell the words "CYCLE / PSYCHO." Often the classes do not know whether I am talking about the same word twice like "Cycle/Cycle" or "Psycho/Psycho," so I have a little fun with this idea since both words sound so much alike. Some members in the audience misspell these words. But we finally get these words on the board spelled correctly. I then ask the class whether they think these two words are related or synonymous. The general consensus is no, but then I announce my disagreement.

Chapter 2

Cycle vs. Psycho

The *American Heritage Dictionary* is used to clarify my argument. This is not to say that other dictionaries could not serve the same purpose. I just happen to own two *American Heritage Dictionaries* that has some sentimental value to me. I acquired the first dictionary, a smaller version, in 1982 when I first began my self-imposed educational process. The second dictionary, a much larger version, was obtained in 1989 while taking college courses in prison. They have provided much assistance to my higher education pursuits that I immensely value.

Before sharing with the class the dictionary definitions of the words "cycle" and "psycho," I encourage members of the class to share what they think these words mean. Many in the class agree that the word "cycle" means to repeat the same pattern of activity over and over again. They also use a hand motion to demonstrate something moving in a circle. I naturally respond that the answer given by the class about the word *c-y-c-l-e* is correct.

I go through the same process with the class concerning the word *p-s-y-c-h-o*. Many in the class defined *psycho* as "crazy." With a little grin, I will often say that I understand why the class so quickly answered with the word "crazy" because most of us have occasionally been called psycho by family members and friends. This comment usually generates some laughter from most in the audience since they recognized the truth in this statement and were able to recall family members or friends saying, "Boy, you're crazy," or "Girl, you're crazy," or "Boy, you're psycho," or "Girl, you're psycho" as a result of some abnormal act or behavior warranting such a declaration. The collective laughter from the audience encourages me to proceed deeper into my presentation with more ease and comfort. The audience becomes friendly and less oppositional; more relaxed, and ready to listen. We have become more like friends, and they are prepared to plunge deeper into discussion with me so together, we can arrive at a common understanding or perception consistent with societal norms. This type of understanding can potentially aid them in recognizing certain unfortunate truths about themselves. It can also aid them in self-modification of character traits they agree are inconsistent with societal norms.

Developing an understanding of perception is an intellectual process, thus a mental exercise. To begin this intellectual process, I start by introducing pertinent excerpts from the dictionary's definition of the word "cycle." It is copied on a transparency, and projected on a screen for the audience to examine. They are asked to offer their individual interpretations of what the definition means to them. The *American Heritage Dictionary*, Second College Edition, defines the word "cycle," in ways consistent with the objectives of my presentation, as follows:

> **cycle**- n. 1. A time interval in which a characteristic, especially a regularly repeated event or sequence of events occurs.
>
> 2. To move in, or as if in, a circle.

Of course, I receive myriad responses from the audience, but, for the most part, they all seem to have the right idea. Most people demonstrate their understanding of the meaning by physically rotating a hand in a circular motion with an index finger extended. I take this matter a step further to provide the audience with a more profound understanding of what most of the individual words in that definition mean. This process is designed to promote the desire to read as well as an interest in critical reading and analytical thinking. It is also designed to encourage reading always with the aid of a dictionary and, if necessary, maps and other geographical materials since reading in this way immensely broadens the readers understanding of nearly any subject.

The first thing I do in this process is to direct the audience's attention to the second part of the definition of the word *cycle*, "To move in, or as if in, a circle." I mention that this particular portion of the definition is obviously self-explanatory and I demonstrate it by moving back to the white board with the dry-erase marker to draw a large circle on the board that reflects the meaning, "To move in, or as if in, a circle." The large blank circle can be found on the last page of this chapter.

Once that part of the definition is clarified, I direct everyone's attention to the dictionary's definition of the word: "A time interval in which a characteristic, especially a regularly repeated event, or sequence of events occurs." This definition is not so self-explanatory to the average unsophisticated mind. I never intentionally try to embarrass anyone, especially in regards to people's intellectual faculties, or the lack thereof. So, I initially ask for volunteers in the audience to take this portion of the definition and break it down to the level that a fifth grader could understand.

Often I get volunteers who do a fairly good job in breaking down this portion of the definition, though not to the required level of understanding. This failure typically occurs because they lack knowledge of the meaning of every word in the sentence; though not one word in that sentence could be defined as very complicated. Each word, in fact, is a very common word that most people should be familiar with.

But that is not the case with my audiences. Some people lack this knowledge of some common words because whenever they do read, they often read without a dictionary. Therefore, before I demonstrate my method of breaking down this sentence, I ask the audience to tell me which one of the words between "time" and "interval" is primary and which one is secondary in their positions in the sentence. This question is just a clever ploy to check the audiences' understanding of grammar. The question also has a therapeutic significance in that its purpose is to promote the importance of language arts. So I take this opportunity to highlight the basic meaning of this portion of the definition of *cycle* found in the first sentence. I utilize a rhetorical criticism method, which I learned in a Ball State University speech communications course. The analogy I often use to break down and explain the profound meaning of the first sentence in the definition of cycle is a clock. A clock is usually positioned somewhere on the wall in the classroom. First, the word "time" is the second word and the second most important word in the sentence. In addition, the clock obviously deals with time. So I use the clock on the wall to help make my point.

The word "interval" is the third word in the sentence but the most important word because, of all the words in the sentence, it defines the word "cycle" most directly. When one considers how the words "time" and "interval" are grammatically juxtaposed in the sentence, "interval" is clearly the noun and "time" is merely an adjective modifying the noun. Since "time" is a mere modifier of the primary word "interval," the grammatical status of the word "time" is secondary to the word "interval." Since most people already know what "time" means, I move on to the next question about the meaning of the word "interval."

I have discovered over and over again that many of the guests in the audience do not have a clue as to the meaning of the word "interval." However, from time to time, someone in the audience did know the definition, and I would offer them an opportunity to share the meaning with the class. Then I am prepared to demonstrate my method of breaking down the definition of the word "cycle" to its fundamental meaning by utilizing the clock on the wall.

Using the clock on the wall as an analogy, I direct the class's attention to the clock and specifically to the numeral twelve at the top and to any one of the three hands on the clock. I tell them to pretend that the numeral "12" represents a particular point on the clock and a starting point. To demonstrate an example of an interval, we move a hand on the clock from the numeral "12" over to the numeral "1." This move, although considerably short, represents an object (hand) moving in a space between two points. The 12 to 1, is a move that technically represents an interval, just as the move from the 1 to the 2 represents another interval. Of course, the 2 to 3 represents another interval. They get the point. Another example of an interval starts at the 12, and goes all the way around to the 12, a move that represents the hand on the clock rotating in a complete circle (space) starting at point "A" and ending at point "A," thus making a complete revolution. This complete revolution of the hand on the clock is an interval as well as a cycle.

I then conduct a brief discussion on the word "characteristic," which is part of the first sentence above. It defines *c-y-c-l-e* and has a role in my use of the clock to make my point. In the above example of the clock, the word "characteristic" functions as a metaphor for the numbers and other markings that are positioned around the clock. This represent specific time periods. It follows that the word "characteristic" is succeeded by the phrases "a regularly repeated event" and "sequence of events" in the aforementioned sentence that further defines c-y-c-l-e.

Pointing to a hand on the clock, I demonstrate how it starts at the 12, and makes a complete revolution around to the 12 again, a process it repeats continuously. I physically demonstrate this because, I never take for granted that everyone in the audience understands the simplest language. At the same time, I explain to the audience the meaning of the phrase "a regularly repeated event." I go on to explain that a "sequence of events" is an event that proceeds in an alphabetical, numeric, or some other previously established order. The purpose of this cumulative demonstration is to establish in the presentation "CYCLE / PSYCHO," precisely how human behaviors, like the hands on a clock, can revolve as "regularly repeated events" and therefore constitute a cycle of events. And, of course, I add the crucial point that if a human being demonstrates a cycle of behaviors construed by societal standards as negative and counter-productive, then those behaviors are "psycho" or crazy.

Ultimately, I explain to my audience that this method of investigating, evaluating, and critiquing language is commonly known in speech communications as "rhetorical criticism."

In fact, I still own the book that was required reading for the rhetorical criticism class I took in 1991, Sonja K. Foss's *Rhetorical Criticism, Exploration & Practice*. Often this book accompanies me to places where I am scheduled to carry out the "CYCLE / PSYCHO" presentation. Whenever I discuss rhetorical criticism in my presentations, I generally display the book to establish that it is categorized in study as a discipline and not a science.

Currently, I use an overhead projector for the words *rhetorical criticism* and *rhetoric* along with the definitions. As I have done previously with the word "cycle" and its definitions, I engage the audience in reading and examining the definition of *rhetorical criticism* and of the several definitions of *rhetoric*. According to Foss, the definitions of the aforementioned words are as follows:

rhetorical criticism- It is the investigation and evaluation of rhetorical acts and artifacts for the purpose of understanding rhetorical processes.

rhetoric- 1. Commonly used to mean empty, bombastic language that has no substance. 2. In other instances, rhetoric is used to mean flowery, ornamental speech that contains an abundance of metaphors and other figures of speech.

rhetoric-   In the discipline of rhetorical criticism means the use of symbols to influence thought and action. Rhetoric is communications; it is simply an old term for what is now commonly called communication.

Though some of the above language may appear a bit complicated to some in the audience, we use simple language and examples in explaining these definitions.

The first part of the definition of rhetorical criticism, "investigation and evaluation…," basically means "the looking into or the probing into" a thing for the purpose of "weighing its value or determining its importance." The second part of the definition, "rhetorical acts and artifacts," means a "live" and "recorded" activity. A rhetorical act is a "live" presentation or performance and not a recorded one. The live act could be a public speech, hip-hop rap, musical performance, or dance. On the other hand, a rhetorical artifact is simply the former "live" performance that has now been recorded on a video, audio mechanism or transcribed in print. The third and final part of the definition, "for the purpose of understanding rhetorical processes," means "a final determination and conclusion of why an act was performed and what effects were produced from it."

The word "rhetoric" has much simpler definitions. One of the first definitions of the word rhetoric commonly refers to empty, bombastic language that has no substance." That is, the use of big words or fantastic language simply for show while possessing very little or no meaning. In layman's terms, "bologna" or boastful talk. (Another definition of the word "rhetoric" involves the use of coded, metaphoric, and symbolic languages or communications.

The word "rhetoric," and how it is applied to rhetorical criticism "means the use of symbols to influence thought and action." I interpret this to mean, for example, the use of emblems/and or copyrighted language such as Nike, Lexus, Cadillac, Chanel, Coach, Gabbana, Gucci, Phat Farm, and Baby Phat which in the commercial world, are designed to influence consumers to purchase those products whether they need them or not. Finally, in the discipline of rhetorical criticism, rhetoric is just "an old term for what is now commonly called communication."

The next order of business is to translate the word p-*s*-*y*-*c*-*h*-*o* into understandable language and clarify its relationship to the word c-y-c-l-e. While we may not find these two words to be fraternal twins, we may discover that they are at least first cousins.

The overall definitions of the word "psycho," when equated with some of our negative behavioral characteristics, has the ability to produce psychopathic implications in many of us, who imagine ourselves remote from it. Therefore, if one should realistically juxtapose their negative behavior with the overall definitions of psycho, then a symbolic mirror may be produced to reflect the similarity between one's behavior and the psychopathic personality, as implied by the overall definitions of psycho. I have determined the word "psycho" to be the most important word between itself and the word "cycle." Reason being, after deciphering the literal definition of *psycho,* using principles of rhetorical criticism, my audience and I discovered that the deciphered meaning of *psycho* represented the primary key for persons to look into their own cycle of behavioral characteristics, and realize that some serious changes must be made within to remove oneself from the psychopathic personality. By doing this, a positive change takes place in their overall behavior. The *American Heritage Dictionary* defines the word "psycho" as follows:

psycho- A psychopath.
Crazy;
Insane

The definition of psycho "appears" to be brief, but as we all know, appearances can be misleading at times. However, if we were to examine just the first word "psychopath" in the definition of *psycho,* we might find that *psycho* has a subtle definition that is far more extensive. Since most people know at least the general meanings of *crazy* and *insane*, I will focus only on the definition of *psychopath.*

> **psychopath**- (n.) A person with a personality disorder, especially one manifested in aggressively antisocial behavior.

You probably know the basic meanings of the words crazy and insane, but defining psychopath is a little more complicated. Most of you, like my usual audiences, probably think of a psychopath as a serial killer, a repeat rapist, or an anti-social maniac of some type. But let us use the principles of rhetorical criticism to decipher the deeper meaning of that term. The class's participation in defining information, arms the class with a sense of ownership of the understanding embraced by the whole group rather than relying exclusively on the facilitator's measure of understanding to arrive at truths. Additionally, the class's participation in the development of an understanding or perception accepted by the whole class instills pride and inspires increased involvement in the teaching process. In deciphering the definition of *psychopath,* the facilitator must gain   the attention of the entire class because this is the most critical place to begin changing the minds of those whose morals are misplaced.

A psychopath is a person afflicted "with a personality disorder." But what constitutes a personality disorder? A personality disorder is quite simply a personality that is out of order, malfunctioning or broken.

The definition mentions that the personality disorder is "especially manifested." The word "especially" is of course synonymous with the word "particularly" and the word "manifest" means to come into existence or become apparent to the sight, mind, or to other human senses. Therefore, when a disordered personality manifests itself it is accompanied by some inappropriate or abnormal behavior.

Next, we must deal with the word aggressively, starting with the root word "aggress," which means to attack or to boldly initiate, a definition that includes the notion of forward progress or movement.

Finally, the word "behavior" is reasonably self-explanatory. Therefore, I will proceed to examine the word "antisocial" in order to fully clarify the meaning of *psychopath*. The major portion of my audience generally agree that the word "antisocial" means someone desiring to be separated, isolated, or secluded from others. If the majority's belief is accurate here, then the "act" of the individual desiring separation from others is naturally construed as an "act" of backward movement, or regression. The word "antisocial" immediately follows the word "aggressively" in the definition of psychopath. A forward action is suggested in the definition of *aggressively,* whereas a backward action is carried in the definition of *antisocial.* Since the definition of *psychopath* involves a human being and it is humanly impossible for a human being to move forward and backward simultaneously, then the purported meaning here of the word "antisocial," as previously stated in the context of the definition of *psychopath*, is inherently and physiologically inaccurate.

Again, following the principles of rhetorical criticism, I perform a different examination of the word "antisocial." I separate the prefix "anti" from the suffix "social" and define them as individual words. I encourage the audience to help in defining these words, and, as usual, we discover that the word "anti" actually means "against" and "social" derives from the word "society." Now we just replace the word "antisocial" with the words "against society" inside the definition of psychopath and then read the definition as follows:

"A psychopath is a person with a personality disorder, especially one manifested in aggressively 'against society' behavior."

When we consider this new version of the definition, a different meaning from the previous emerges, and thus the decoded interpretation of the literal definition seems more logical. The class concludes that "against society behavior" entails behavior that society deems abnormal, inappropriate, deviant, or criminal--behavior that ranges from something as apparently harmless as habitual traffic offenses to something as heinous as robbery, child molestation, rape, or murder. This analytical conclusion typically brings the entire class to the realization that many of their habitual behaviors may very well be psychopathic.

If through this analysis you have come to realize that you have behaved in ways that could be labeled psychopathic, then it is probably a good time to try to adjust your former perception of yourself and begin the process of transforming yourself into someone who will not be considered antisocial or psychopathic. I cannot promise that the process will be an easy or a painless one, but you must engage in it if you want to improve your perception of the world and the way you think and behave in it. At the end of this painful but necessary process, you will be a better person, a person who will have an easier time integrating once more into society.

Chapter 3

Habitual Negative and Counter-Productive Behaviors

Having established the kinship between the words "cycle" and "psycho" by comparing their individual definitions and functions, the facilitator moves on to demonstrate to the class exactly what habitual negative and counter-productive behavior looks like. This is accomplished by the step-by-step construction of a cycle of such behavioral characteristics aided by a pre-drawn circle as shown on the previous page.

Returning to the circle, I write a number of words that reflect my own thinking and behavior patterns during the time that I was in a psycho cycle.

I tell the class that I will place the words that reflect my own habitual negative and counter-productive thinking and behavior patterns around the interior of the circle at points similar to where the numbers on a clock appear. I then assemble the words one at a time and in a clockwise fashion as I methodically share certain experiences about how a particular word played a role in the history of my life. For example, when I suffered from low self-esteem I will share the whole experience with the class so that they understand how I arrived at that particular stage in my life. As I list the words around the interior, I would say to the class, "Some people in this room will recognize certain unfortunate words relating to my history of character flaws and relate these same words to their own character blemishes." I also inform the class that I suspect at least three basic personalities exist in this class:

1.) Those who would openly admit that they share a particular character flaw I write about myself in the circle
2.) Those who would adamantly conceal their character flaws from others here
3.) Those who would like to share their character flaws with the facilitator but not with their classmates.

Whenever I write in one of those words that reflect my own misguided thinking, the first personality group generally expresses some form of open acknowledgement that they share that particular character flaw. The second personality group, which seemed more reserved and private in demeanor, has the tendency to exhibit a slight flinch on their countenance or involuntarily look away. This second personality group is extremely private and do not want anyone, not even the speaker to know their personal business or what their flaws may be. Then there is the third group that displayed observable signals that they desire to admit their flaws to the facilitator only. To the latter group I suggest that I do in fact have a way for them to admit their flaws to me without others knowing, and that is by merely looking directly at me and raising their eyebrows a couple of times and I would in turn return a private acknowledgement.

Depending on your personality type, you may be willing to acknowledge our shared flaws when you talk with your friends. You may be willing only to acknowledge them to yourself, or you may resist confronting these aspects of your own "psycho" behavior. That last response may protect your feelings and your sense of security, but it will not help you to transform yourself so that you can escape that cycle of psycho behavior and thinking.

Before I write the first word describing one of my previous behaviors in the interior of that large circle, I share a brief story about myself. I explain to the class how the behavior, relating to the word affected me very early, and the adverse impact it had on my life. The same procedure is followed with each word prior to writing it in the circle. Finally, the last set of words is used inside the circle to complete the picture of bad behavior in its totality and it has always been my hope that all in attendance would benefit from it.

Chapter 4

Low Self-Esteem

I begin this portion of the presentation with a discussion about my childhood. As the 8th of 13 children born to my wonderful and dedicated parents, Betty Lou Walters-Curtis-Tinnin and Richard Alexander Tinnin, I grew up wearing a lot hand-me-downs from my older siblings. Other items were purchased from Goodwill Stores, the Salvation Army, or donated by our neighbors or by the church our family attended. Around 1961, when I was about ten, I was attending the nearby Indianapolis Public School #42.

My late parents were born in November 1917 and were wedded in January 1936. Early in the marriage, my mother, worked several years for the United States Army Finance Center in Indianapolis, Indiana. Later, of course, she became a fulltime housewife because she was unable to work outside the home and care for so many children at the same time.

My mother was also a devout Christian, a Sunday school teacher, Bible teacher, and an Ordained Mother in the church, who spent several hours per day several days a week at the church. I cannot recall ever seeing her use tobacco, alcoholic beverages, or drugs and cannot even recall hearing many bad words coming from her mouth. Nevertheless, she was not a "punk" mom. To my knowledge, she would not allow any of her children, to intimidate her or disrespect any adult without serious consequences. She was the enforcer in the home, and when her punishment did not measure up to the nature of the violation, then my father would step in with his measure of corporal discipline, at least for the sons.

My father did administer some very painful discipline at times. I was an exceptionally problematic child and often got myself in new trouble before I could even get   out of the old one. As a result, my father would sometimes increase the pain because I was such a regular violator. I still do not know exactly what was going on in my mind then that influenced me so often to be such a hard-headed fool, especially at such an early age. Maybe I resented following instructions from persons in authority, or maybe I simply wanted to do whatever I wanted to do. Whatever its source, this way of thinking and acting apparently followed me into adulthood. Nevertheless, my father was an extremely strong and responsible man, as I mentioned previously, and he supported all his children long into their 40s, 50s, 60s, and even the 70s in a couple of cases. My resilient mother passed away after 65 years, and my superman father passed away 22 days shy of his 91st birthday in 2008.

Many of my classmates at School #42 were apparently from families who could afford new and fashionable attire. My family situation obviously did not allow such luxuries due to the great number of siblings and the fact that my father was the only financial provider in the home. But though my clothes were always clean and ironed, the so-called "more fortunate students," in my classroom were not always considerate of my feelings. Often they would mock my old and sometimes unfashionable clothes. The irony of this situation was that most of my classmates at School #42 were of African descent. Nevertheless, the social class struggle within the school was uncomfortably similar to what was going on at that time that had led to the civil rights movement outside the school.

Then to compound my mental confusion about the nature of human interactions, my family's church was also predominantly attended by people of African descent. But in spite of that, all the divine characters painted on the walls inside the church or in photographs were images of people that were of European descent (commonly called white people). At the same time, outside the church, white supremacy permeated the society and it perpetrated oppression and violence against people of hue (color) in particular. I began to perceive the church on one hand, as an institution of love and peace among peoples of the world as well as a place to revere divinity. On the other hand, it seemed to be an institution of subtle white domination similar to the overt white domination reflected in the society right outside the doors of the church.

The so-called "more fortunate students" bad-mouthing my inexpensive clothes and shoes did not bother me during my pre-adolescence. However, it bothered me later when my body began to experience the physiological metamorphosis of puberty. When I reached the maturity of puberty, the teasing and taunts from other students about my clothes began to bother, embarrass, and upset me. Still today, this inequality in dress and fashion plagues many young people in the same way it did me. Similarly, it distracts them from achieving their greatest academic potential. This is the primary reason I applaud the current Superintendent of Indianapolis Public Schools, Dr. Eugene White, for taking the bold step of instituting an affordable dress code for students in the school district.

The people who are the poorest in society probably suffer from low self-esteem more than any other group in society. Economic deprivation is likely the outstanding cause of low self-esteem among the poor and they more than others, have benefited from the recent dress code because it substantially diminished the cultural pressure brought to bear on those less fortunate students to compete with their more fortunate peers in stylish and expensive name-brand apparel.

The mockery and teasing I endured regarding my outdated clothes affected me very deeply at that point in my life because I had begun to pursue intimate relations with some of the girls in school and my outdated clothes turned most of them off. I was dealing with a serious testosterone issue and had grown bored with masturbation. Only physical relations with an animate female, I told myself, would gratify my needs.

I desired to establish a close relationship with a popular and attractive female in the school that had the likelihood to overshadow and diminish the unfavorable attention that had been attributed to my character by my peers. Since I failed in every attempt to secure the affections of a desirable female, I decided that I needed to add something to my person that would help me attract such a desirable prize. So, like many young people during the 1960s, I turned to the television set to discover prominent role models to emulate among the movie stars, athletes, and entertainers.

I was not fascinated with any athletes or movie stars, but I was fascinated with a number of entertainers, particularly singers like The Temptations, The Four Tops, The Beach Boys, The Beatles, Elvis Presley, and Jackie Wilson. Emulating an entertainer seemed more attainable to someone less fortunate like me. The common understanding in the African-American community was that many entertainers were previously street corner crooners who were discovered by someone influential and introduced to people with the power to help them achieve public acclaim, financial success, and celebrity status. Furthermore, I noticed how excited and wild many women in the audience acted while accomplished male vocalists were performing and how aggressively these women approached the stage as though they would ravish the singers' bodies if the women could only lay hands on them.

When entertainers like Elvis Presley, The Beatles, The Beach Boys, Chuck Berry, James Brown, and The Temptations, and several others with "straight hair" performed on stage, the women would practically go wild and seemingly lose their minds in excitement. These women were mesmerized by the entertainers' vocals, songs and good looks, part of those good looks, I felt, had to do with the entertainers' "straight hair." Whenever an entertainers' straight hair fell over the eyes during a performance, the excitement of the ladies seemed to increase. I really liked that and imagined myself as an entertainer basking in the sensual attention of the ladies. I relished being on the receiving end of such attention. As a result, I settled on entertainers to emulate in hopes of corralling such attention.

After evaluating a number of entertainers and taking into consideration the racial climate at that time, I determined that Elvis Presley was the best candidate for me. It was definitely rare at that time to see people of hue (color) on television at all. Every now and then, entertainers of African descent like James Brown, Chuck Berry, The Four Tops, and The Temptations would make an appearance for some musical performance. Otherwise, people of hue almost never appeared on television unless the role was a janitor, butler, chauffeur, or some other menial occupation.

Henceforth, I began to take an exceptional interest in Elvis Presley because he was extremely popular and received a lot of television time. I wanted to observe every moment, live or recorded when he performed on a television variety show, interviewed on a talk show, or acted in a movie. During the late 1950s and early 1960s, Elvis was just sensational for my young, impressionable mind. He possessed exactly what I craved in my life at that time: an attractive and sexual image that a lot of women desired. Of course, I was much too young at that time to believe that grown women would desire me in that way, but it was not far-fetched for girls in my peer group to display such sentiments. However, it was not just the image of Elvis that I was impressed with, I also desired to achieve the kind of fame he enjoyed. Now, I know that this particular ambition was far-fetched, but I dreamed it and imagined that I could achieve it.

During my adolescence, I started practicing the lyrics of Elvis's songs and his stage theatrics upstairs in the bathroom of my parents' home. I would shut the door of the bathroom so that family members could not see what I was doing, hoping they would just think I was using the facilities for hygienic purposes. But I was actually standing in the mirror watching myself singing the lyrics of many of Elvis's songs as my hips simulated the gyrations he was widely noted for. I would then imagine the excitement of the women growing louder and louder. That is exactly what took place when the real Elvis was performing. I pretended so much to be like Elvis that I shook my head back and forth, as my emotions heightened and I got more deeply involved in the singing. As Elvis got emotionally involved in his singing, he would often shake his head back and forth, causing the long, silky, straight black hair just above his forehead to fall down over his eyes, and then, with one of his hands, he would casually swipe the hair away from his eyes. That movement alone would cause the women to scream even louder. So naturally, I expected my black hair to fall over my eyes when I shook my head as I sang, and I would subsequently swipe the hair away. Unfortunately, for me, I had a wooly afro that remained in place no matter how hard I shook my head.

I could not psychologically afford to allow that wooly hair situation to go unresolved, especially if I expected to become a genuine Elvis imitator. I reasoned that I could not be Elvis if I could not get my hair to move on head-shaking command. Coincidentally, around that same time I had observed my sister Lois using a hot iron comb that she had heated on the kitchen stove to press her afro until it became straight like the hair on a Caucasian person. If I followed the same procedure, I told myself, the problem with my wooly hair would then be solved. Therefore, I retrieved the hot comb when Lois was finished with it, and straightened my hair.

Once I completed my hair straightening, I resumed the Elvis Presley performance in the mirror. I was immensely satisfied now that I was able to cause my hair to fall over my eyes just by rhythmically shaking my head as I sang some of my favorite Elvis songs. This enabled me to perform more like the real Elvis. I felt then like I was truly on the road to victory. Of course, my eagerness to have my hair straightened was not an unusual phenomenon at that time in the African American male community. In fact, during that era an assortment of hair-straightening techniques emerged in the African-American male community, e.g., the Murray process, the pressing of the hair with an iron-straightening comb, perms, Jeri curls, S-curls, and various chemical hair relaxers.

But just as soon as I thought I had everything I needed to be Elvis, another problem arose. I was too dark to be Elvis Presley. Oh my God! I had gotten so very close to being where I needed to be, and now a new problem. I had to do something about that. So I began to rub hard, not to cause any damage to my skin but to rid it of its pigmentation (color). Of course, that technique failed. As with the issue of "good hair" and "bad hair," it was not unusual at that time for some people of color to detest their pigmentation because being Black "was not cool." It was not until the late 1960s when the Godfather of Soul, James Brown, produced the song "I am Black and I am Proud" that being Black became cool.

Sometime after my fascination with Elvis Presley had faded, I developed a new attraction to a European (commonly called white) musical group from England, the Beatles. Obviously, I was not alone, because I was aware that a number of other African Americans were also fascinated with the Beatles. A number of the teenagers in my peer group were not shy about their Beatle mania.

That strange attitude of mine developed when I was an adolescent into my early teen years. Other people like the accomplished entertainer Michael Jackson, apparently suffered from a similar mentality. With his millions, however, Jackson could afford to alter his natural physical appearance more than I could. Straightening my hair was the only change in my physical appearance I could finance. If I had Jackson's finances maybe I would have altered my physical appearance to the extent that he did. A person reading this or hearing me explain all this during a public presentation might initially think that Michael Jackson and I both were, at best, eccentric, or at worst, crazy. But I cannot see much difference between people who want to remove the pigmentation (color) from their flesh and other people who burn themselves in the hot sun on the beach or in a tanning bed hoping to give their body a richer, darker pigmentation. Both groups are dissatisfied with the natural complexion of their flesh and seek to artificially alter it.

The same principle can be applied to persons who have their flesh tattooed. What on earth would influence a person to have their body tattooed with all sorts of images? Maybe they think that the body would not look right without the tattoos. Perhaps their body is bland or dull without them. In this kind of thinking, the body lacks life without tattoos. Any time a person looks in the mirror and is discontented with the image he or she sees and therefore decides to alter it or to have it altered to make it more pleasing, that person is evidently suffering from low self-esteem. When a person looks into the mirror and detests his or her appearance then the person does not like his or her self.

Why do Avon and Revlon sell an astronomical amount of so-called "beauty products?" The answer is pretty simple. Much of the female population looked into their mirrors and determined that they would not look good enough unless they modify their facial features with "beauty products." What make-up actually does is give women an exaggerated appearance. I am not trying to badmouth the notion of a woman wearing make-up; I am just analyzing the things people do to alter their natural appearance when they are dissatisfied with it. And despite whatever opposition I encounter as a result, I insist that some low self-esteem issues exist within these individuals. Most people look in the mirror and perceive many different things about themselves: they are too tall, too short, too fat, or too skinny, or they have unpleasant features, bad hair, or a fabulous complexion. Whatever physical features a person is born with; when that person looks in the mirror and determines that those very features diminish his or her beauty then I would submit that such a person has some self-esteem issues.

During my teen years and early adulthood, I was not profoundly aware of the effects of negative self-perception, but today I have a much better understanding of how negatively I perceived myself. It was low self-esteem. I did not like myself. I was discontented because of the false perception that I was not good enough to be accepted by many of my prominent classmates and other peers. I consequently internalized as truths the negative judgments of my former classmates and other peers. As a young person, whenever I looked in the mirror and saw the physical image bestowed on me at birth, I found no love in that reflection. Obviously, I suffered from low self-esteem.

The confusing mental images that developed in my mind because of all those European (commonly called white) religious figures depicted in pictures at church were echoed in my experience of public education where all the pictures on the walls in classrooms were of famous European Americans who were U.S. Presidents, inventors, or military heroes. School textbooks were not much different other than there were a few people of hue pictured in them, always as menial workers or slaves. I rejected this notion of white supremacy with its dual intimidating influences of power and oppression. But though I did not allow it to dominate me, I did allow it to influence me during the 1960s. And, of course, in a profound and damaging way, it influenced people of hue across the United States and around the world. Sometimes obviously and sometimes in a more subtle way this pervasive notion of white supremacy manifested itself in practically every facet of human activity. Consequently, I parted ways prematurely with both church and school.

On the following page is a large circle with the words "low self-esteem" written on the inside. "Low self-esteem" at the 12 o'clock position inside the circle represents the root cause of my negative and counter-productive c-y-c-l-e of thinking and behaving.

Low Self-Esteem

Chapter 5

Illiteracy

Now we have "low self-esteem" in position as the starting point of my psycho cycle. Following that of course, is illiteracy.

My classmates, especially those more fortunate economically, played a big role in discouraging my attendance at school by their ridicule of the old-fashioned clothing my parents bought from the Goodwill and Salvation Army and the worn clothes handed down to me by my elder siblings, church members, and other benefactors outside the home.

From the time I went to kindergarten until approximately the 4th or 5th grades, I pretty much enjoyed being in school every day primarily because of the camaraderie and fun shared by those of us who were class clowns and who basically came to school for the entertainment we unofficially provided. I was enthusiastically active in classroom antics, but lethargic when it came to academics. Besides, I actually hated school for two basic reasons: 1.) The frequent taunts from some of my classmates, which made me uncomfortable and unhappy while in school; and 2.), the promotion of white supremacy that was subtly intertwined in the academic curriculum, especially during the 1960s when people of hue were being indoctrinated to accept an inferior station in life. The taunts from my peers and the biased educational system both caused me to feel bad about myself. The educational system, in addition, did nothing to make me feel good or proud about my African American culture and heritage. Back then, I definitely could not have expressed these sentiments in these terms, but that was precisely how I felt. As a result of all these factors, I felt that I had to devise some way to make school tolerable for at least seven hours. I found clowning around in class, creating classroom antics that would elicit laughter from others, and simply "acting" crazy periodically, provided a comforting form of escape from a situation that produced so much discomfort and mental pain for me.

Nothing my teachers said or did; no visual images and no language displayed around the classrooms or in textbooks were able to motivate me to excel academically. I was able to earn Cs in language arts, but in math, science, and history I failed miserably. I attended school practically every day, but I completed very few of my classroom assignments. Soon I began to get so far behind in my classroom assignments, and lost so much confidence in my ability to produce accurate results, that I actually surrendered to academic failure. Thus, my poor academic performance resulted in the repetition of several grades. Those failures caused frustration and despair to take root in my demeanor. I did not surrender to them absolutely though. I found solace in the discovery that I was not alone in this predicament.

At the same time a number of other students, particularly males, in my classroom and other classrooms of the same grade level, were apparently experiencing the same discouraging feelings about the school curriculum. This shared dissatisfaction created a sense of commonality, and thus friendships and collaborations developed among these like-minded individuals. Ultimately, we decided that all of us hated school and even a few of the staff members. We realized that the only reason we continued to show up at school was that we were not old enough by law to drop out. But though the law did not permit us to drop out of school physically, the law could not prevent us from dropping out of school mentally. Consequently, students like Anthony Ballard, Anthony Burris, Anthony Folley, Anthony Owens, the twins Bernice and Ernest McClain, Clay Byers, D'Coby McGuire, Frank Harris, Gregory Resnover, Jesse Lester, Jesse McElwain, John Foster, Keith Lewis, Larry King, Lawrence Harris, Lonnie Belmar, Nathaniel Allen, William Mitchell, William Smith and I, all basically dropped out of school mentally, while our physical bodies continued to occupy a chair in the classroom. But the truth behind this mental truancy was my illiteracy.

I abhorred the idea of reading; the literature as well as the book covers that I was exposed to as a youth in the public school and the church; were quite discouraging to me. My mind was not motivated to explore their contents. The cumulative pictures displayed within their pages told a demeaning and painful story of its own, about people of hue versus those who lack hue (Caucasians). In addition, loud verbal exchanges I was privy to hear between the well-read folks concerning the contents of the Holy Bible and many school textbooks only compounded my distaste for reading. Ultimately, I concluded that the achievement of functional literacy was a painful prospect. My socio-economic situation at that time was already causing me sufficient discomfort; therefore, I remained functionally illiterate, at least until I decided to do something about it. But it would take another twenty years before I actually acknowledged that I was seriously illiterate.

Illiteracy is the second characteristic in my c-y-c-l-e of negative and counter-productive thinking and behavior. So now, I write the word "illiterate" in the position next to "low self-esteem."

Low Self-Esteem
  Illiteracy

Chapter 6

Gang

The many negative comments my classmates made about my outdated clothes did much to cause the discomfort I experienced in school. That discomfort was psychologically painful. When a person encounters pain, he or she instinctively resort to ways of alleviating that pain as quickly as possible, even by drastic means if necessary. So to block out the discomfort I experienced as a result of cruel words hurled at me by classmates, I often resorted to becoming a comedian with a humorous focus on anything or anybody except me. In fact, portraying the role of a comedian to deflect the painful feeling of inadequacy I experienced as a result of the unfavorable comments from my classmates regarding my person, became so ingrained in my personality that even today I often incite laughter during large gatherings among friends and family. I relied on this tactic so frequently that it ultimately elevated me to the status of class clown. This tactic inevitably became contagious among a number of latent clowns in class, because very quickly they began to reveal themselves as such. Many of them were actually some of my most candid detractors and antagonists.

Humans are social animals by nature and have a human need to interact with other human beings. Failing that, they will turn to animals or other living creatures of the earth. The same principle applies, of course, to illiterates or dummies who are, after all, human beings. For the sake of clarification, let us define the words "illiterate" and "dummy." We sometimes hear a word used so often by others that we form a basic understanding of its meaning without ever looking in a dictionary. For most, words have multiple definitions, but we will examine only the definitions as they apply in the context of the current discussion. My *American Heritage Dictionary* defines *illiterate* and *dummy*, as follows:

> **illiterate**- adj. 1. a. Unable to read and write.
> b. Having little or no formal education.
>
> **dummy**- n. 1. An imitation of a real or original object, intended to be used as a practical substitute...
> 3. A stupid person.

The students discussed above did in fact have little or no formal education at that time and regularly behaved foolishly in class; therefore, they meet the dictionary definitions of these words. Dummies in the classroom are generally shunned by the studious pupils because they are opposites and share little in common. The studious ones are often involved in classroom assignments and progressively improving their grades while the dummies in class are often preoccupied with non-classroom activities. Since it is in our nature to interact with other human beings, it follows that dummies are not content to sit idly dumb in the classroom from 8:00 a.m. until 3:00 p.m. Misery loves company, and so do dummies. Since the dummy is unlikely to get involved in any classroom assignments to occupy his or her class time constructively, he or she will need something to occupy class time unless sleeping in class is allowed.

Usually when people are not involved in positive activities, they are typically involved in negative ones. It is an old adage that "An idle mind is the devil's workshop." Dummies will covertly seek out other dummies in the class in hopes of establishing some rapport that might catapult them into some stimulating and mischievous activity that is usually not class-related.

Such activity, though stimulating, is often quite negative, but it is the stimulation that keeps the dummies awake. Dummy relationships generally begin with two dummies. It then gradually multiplies when other latent dummies become interested in the activities of the original dummies. This determines if it is safe for them to enter the deviltries. Soon more and more latent dummies enter the foolishness and bring along their personal antics and class disruptions; thus, a significant army of dummies are formed in the classroom. The dummies are, however, intelligent enough that they soon recognize that there are a significant number of them in the classroom; their brilliant minds begin to turn for the worst.

Their counter-productive behaviors not only disrupt normal classroom productivity but also affect the minds and attitudes of everyone directly or indirectly associated with them, including the teacher. Those present in the classroom during the misbehavior are, of course, the people most directly affected. The people indirectly affected by these class clowns are family and friends because the personality of the perpetrator inherently follows him wherever he goes.

My fellow class clowns and I started to perceive ourselves collectively as an organized group of hoodlum-minded individuals, without a label. Besides, we had not paid enough attention in class to know how to spell the word "organization." Therefore, we identified ourselves by the four-letter word "gang," which was much easier to spell. That word was commonly the preferred identification that loosely organized youth groups, like ours, subscribed to when I was a youth. And by identifying ourselves as a gang, we began the process of producing a gang mentality.

Now let us look at the definition of the word "gang" and then add the suffix "ster" and examine those two words together to determine the basic mentality of a person who identifies with a gang in the context of the above discussion. The dictionary defines the words *gang* and *gangster* as follows:

> **gang-** n. 2. A group of criminals or hoodlums who band together for mutual protection and profit.
> 3. A group of adolescents who band together, especially a group characterized by delinquency.
>
> **gangster-** n. A member of an organized group of criminals; racketeer.

As these definitions suggest, through our friendship and clownishness, a segment of the classroom became what could be construed as a gang. When the behavior of individuals or groups is consistent with the dictionary's definition of *gang* or *gangster*, it would be wise for the individual or group to view themselves accordingly; then acknowledge the deviancy in their behavior if positive changes are to occur. Wisdom, of course, is typically in short supply in such groups.

Here again I return to the circle to write another word inside the large circle. This time the word *gang* is placed at the 3 o'clock position inside the circle just below the word *illiterate*.

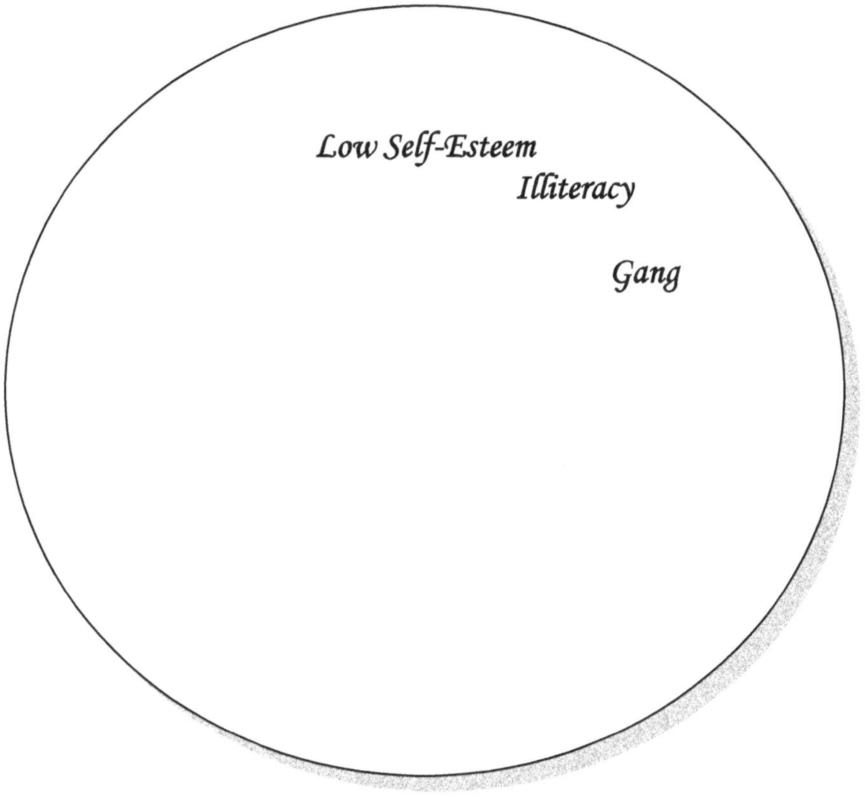
Low Self-Esteem
Illiteracy
Gang

Chapter 7

Thug Life

It is a bold and counter-productive act for an individual, a group, or an organization to publicly announce at this present time in history that they represent a gang or take part in gang activities. In addition, past and recent public safety issues relating to the proliferation of illicit drugs and violence, and the simultaneous terrorist attacks that occurred on September 11, 2001 in New York, Pennsylvania, and Washington, D.C., all loudly proclaim gang affiliation. This would be a valid reason for law enforcement agencies to pay extreme and perpetual attention to such a group of individuals.

Many negative connotations emanate from the word "gang," as established in chapter 6, and that's possibly the reason some individuals and groups attach substitute words that are similar, yet seem to have less blatant connotations. They do this when claiming their street credibility. Little do these individuals realize that, in most cases, many of the substitute words have more blatancy and are more sinister in their connotations than the words they originate from.

These days I often hear young people, particularly teens, boast to others that: "I am a savage," "I am a goon," or "I am a beast," as if these labels are something to be proud of and deserving of honor and respect. I often wonder whether these individuals really understand the meaning of those words.

The dictionary defines them as follows:

savage- adj. 1. Not domesticated or cultivated; wild. 2. Not civilized; barbaric.

goon- n. 1. (Informal.) A thug hired to intimidate or harm opponents. 2. (Slang.) A stupid or oafish person.

beast- n. 1. a. An animal as distinguished from man. 3. A brutal or vile person.

Language is quite powerful, and the language a person attaches to a thing affects the way the person perceives that thing. Judging from the three words listed above, what other more demeaning and depraved words in the English vocabulary could a so-called human being, attach to his or her self? It should be shameful for any person to take pride in identifying his or her self in such terms, yet some young people today seem to relish terms that reflect self-denigration and self-destruction.

During the Tupac Shakur era, for instance, it was widely popular for young people to identify themselves as thugs. So, I decided to make the word *thug* part of the original presentation that I had created as a contract employee for IDOC, to present to offenders incarcerated in Indiana correctional facilities. I figured that a number of offenders at that time were part of the culture that defined themselves as thugs. Being aware of the power of words, I felt that I could rely on the actual definition of *thug* to discourage their perception of themselves in those terms.

I believe that I had read somewhere in Sonja K. Foss's book *Rhetorical Criticism* where she stated that "The words that we attach to any person, place, or thing affect the way we perceive and treat that person, place, or thing." So, if then, I attach a friendly word like *fabulous* to how I identify a certain person, it is likely I will treat the person in a friendly and fabulous way. However, if I attach an adversarial identification, like *enemy*, to a certain person, then it is highly probable I will treat the person in a mean and distrustful way. The same principle applies when a person attaches a negative or positive word that describes how the person sees his or her self. The person will treat self according to the nature of words the person attaches to himself. The word *thug*, therefore, is likely to have a damaging effect on a person's perception of himself.

Let us consider how the dictionary defines the word *thug,* and then let us put this word in its proper perspective. The dictionary defines the word *thug* as follows:

thug- n. 1. A cutthroat or ruffian; hoodlum.
2. One of a band of professional assassins formerly active in northern India.

And consider, further, how the dictionary defines those three initial words that define *thug*:

cutthroat- n. 1. One who cuts throats; murderer.
2. An unprincipled and ruthless person.

ruffian- n. A tough or rowdy fellow; a thug or gangster.

hoodlum- n. A tough, destructive young man. A gangster; thug.

Here it is evident that the definition of *thug* is directly akin to the word *gangster* and the implied violence that accompanies it. People may boast about being a thug or simply identify themselves as thugs, but the implications also include being a cutthroat and murderer. In fact, all the above words defined in this chapter, in addition to *gang* and *gangster* in the previous chapter, have violent implications. Therefore, if a person defines his or her self in the words mentioned in this chapter and the previous one, then that person's character and behavior embodies the violent attributes inherent in those words. I have certainly never known or heard of a gang member, gangster, or thug who embraced the principle of "non-violence" as advocated and espoused by renowned historical personalities such as Mohandas Gandhi and the Reverend Dr. Martin Luther King, Jr.

For example, when one considers the high homicide rate in Indianapolis, Indiana, and who are the victims and perpetrators of those homicides, one may very well discover that the "thug mentality" is the primary culprit. Furthermore, it is the same scenario in every major city throughout the United States. According to a newspaper article published on January 12, 2009, in the *Indianapolis Star*, "the city of Indianapolis and county of Marion experienced 123 homicides in the year 2008. Out of 123 homicides recorded for that year 71% of the homicide victims were age 34 and younger; about 65% were of African descent; and 75% died by gunshot." In that article Dionne Leslie, the Executive Director of the Christamore House Family and Community Center, states that: "Poverty, drugs, and other social problems are devastating within the Black community." "Young Black men," Leslie goes on to say, "can fall into a cycle of dropping out of school, running the streets, selling drugs and committing other crimes." It is surely common knowledge that those who murder people of African descent in cities like Indianapolis are overwhelmingly other people of African descent.

In an earlier *Indianapolis Star* article (February 26, 2006) titled "Symposium Explores Ways to Cut Black-on-Black Crime," the Indianapolis Police Department issued an official statistical report that included a statement that "The majority of homicides in Indianapolis are Black-on-Black crimes, accounting for 57 or 65 percent of the 88 killings recorded in 2005."

People of African descent in America find it relatively easy to murder one another as a direct result of the "Willie Lynch syndrome" that has been in effect since 1712. William Lynch, a man of European descent who owned slaves on a plantation in the West Indies, was also renowned for his expertise in the control of slaves and was often sought out by other slave owners for advice on methods of effectively controlling slaves. Copies of a document titled "The Infamous Willie Lynch Letter" are floating around all over the United States today that purportedly contain a speech that Willie Lynch delivered in the state of Virginia to an audience of slave owners. It outlines the most effective and long-lasting methods of controlling slaves.

The speech affirms that if his instructions for controlling slaves are followed properly then the effects on the slaves could last for hundreds of years and maybe thousands. I do not have the space or the stomach to insert the entire speech here, but I would advise everyone to get a copy of that document and read it several times and then pass it on to anyone else who would like to read it. Lynch states that if the slave owners will exploit the physical differences between the slaves; such as, shades of skin, texture of hair, physical size, age, and location to influence the slaves to distrust, envy, and despise other slaves, thus, using their difference to distrust, envy, and hate one another. This will keep the slaves in conflict so that they will never unite to free themselves.

The same attitudes and mentalities persist today among many of the people of African descent in America. This kind of thinking is demeaning and deplorable to say the least, and it is primarily responsible for the violence people of African descent perpetrate against each other on a daily basis.

Despite the fact that people of the same racial group are inherently alike physically and culturally, some individuals within that racial group, without meaningful cause, manufacture other physical ways such as gang membership, clothing colors, and locations to differentiate themselves from others within that group and then use those meaningless differences as a justification to create rivalries. A recent example of this mentality took place in Chicago, Illinois, on September 24, 2009, when 16-year-old Derrion Albert, an African American male, was viciously kicked and beaten to death with a wooden plank by several other young African American males, all captured on video via a bystander's camera phone. Albert, a sophomore honor roll student on his way home from school, was a bystander and not part of the fight between two groups feuding at that time. This case made national news. The *Indianapolis Star* published an Associated Press report on September 29, 2009, that stated: "His [Derrion Albert's] death was the latest addition to a rising toll," referring to the more than 30 students killed in Chicago the year before. The recent episodes of violence perpetrated against youth in Chicago have grown at an alarming rate.

The rampant violence that persons of African descent inflict on one another throughout America is partly derived from the learned hatred they have for their own race that has trickled down from the old slave system. But even more important, the people who commit such crimes have learned to hate themselves, though they might never admit that. Such a negative perception of one's own race and self is an unmitigated slave mentality. While I am an avid fan of old school music, and tasteful hip hop, rap and great beats; another cause for the perpetuation of the slave mentality among young African Americans, especially certain rap artists of the hip hop generation, can be linked to the identification of themselves with the names of infamous European Americans such as John Gotti, Al Capone, and Scarface Nelson, and the identification of themelves as a "beast," "savage," "goon," "gangster," or a "thug."

The use of these labels and infamous names is merely some unconscious attempt to disguise a mentality that is akin to slavery. A person who conceives himself to be a beast, savage, gangster, or thug is likely to display an animalistic attitude towards others. These same labels and infamous names also breed self-hate, and could possibly materialize into violence against others who may be the focus of that hatred. Therefore, it would not be surprising if a person, who assumes an alias like C-Murder, is eventually suspected of, or charged with murder. The language that we attach to any person, place, or thing affects the way we perceive that person, place, or thing, and are likely to affect the way we treat that person, place, or thing as stated by Sonja K. Foss.

I write the words *thug life* on the right side and inside the large circle just below the word *gang*. Then I immediately prepare to discuss the succeeding matter, i.e. violence. I now proceed to discuss the succeeding link in the circle.

Low Self-Esteem
Illiteracy

Gang

Thug Life

Chapter 8

Violence

Violence is actually a characteristic any person can possess. One does not have to belong to a gang, or be a gangster, or a thug, to be violent. Many typical hard-working adults in America, male and female, blue and white collar, do not belong to a gang. Nevertheless, they physically and/or emotionally abuse their spouses, children, neighbors, or other people and animals. Such people are obviously violent. Violence seems to permeate our society in many forms. In fact, human beings seem to be in love with violence. Consider how much violence is part of many of the activities we enjoy every day: television, video games, ultimate fighting, boxing, wrestling, hockey, football, and soccer. Many of our youth in this generation have been raised on violent video games, television, and movies. They learn very early that violence can be quite pleasurable and fulfilling.

Violence does not entail only a physical act even though, of course, physical violence is the most repulsive form. Some people may think that verbal attacks such as teasing, ridicule, and defaming are trivial and do not constitute forms of violence. But indeed, they do constitute a form of violence. The dictionary defines various forms of violence as follows:

violence- n. 1. Physical force exerted for the purpose of violating, damaging, or abusing; crimes of violence.

4. The abusive or unjust exercise of power.

5. Abuse or injury to meaning, content, or intent; do violence to a text.

It surely should not be a surprise to anyone that violence includes unjust ridicule, defaming, teasing, and taunting others. These acts are psychologically violent and offensive and can potentially cause intense emotional harm to the person targeted. In my youth, when I was subjected to the teasing and taunts of my classmates about my outdated clothing, the low self-esteem I suffered was primarily produced by that verbal, non-physical violence. Some sense of power was apparently exerted by certain students who were better situated economically than other students were, myself included. People who shared my situation were significantly deprived economically. Those who were economically privileged used their perceived power to abuse and culturally oppress those who were less fortunate. This sort of behavior by those of superior economic status is obviously a form of oppression and consequently violence.

Eventually I assimilated into the antagonistic culture of the classroom and started verbally attacking other students I perceived as inferior to me; that way, I deflected the violence away from me onto others in the classroom. That marked the advent of my violent behavior. I should mention that I was already familiar with some form of teasing and taunting as experienced between my siblings and me. However, that teasing and taunting was done purely out of love and fun, as a way to escape the boredom and monotony we suffered since our parents restricted us to the home most days. Ill will and animosity did not exist between any of my siblings. My first experience with physical violence was from the many beatings I earned from my parents.

Of course, like most other behaviors we become addicted to because they provide temporary escape from other pain, my periodic verbal violence against my classmates became common. As time progressed so did the urge to do actual physical violence. I started to use violence against others as a cover to hide the fears and weaknesses in me that I did not want others to see. Shortly thereafter, my behavior graduated to bullying. I began to selectively choose individuals among our peer group, who I perceived to be weaker or physically inferior. They were challenged to a physical confrontation in the presence of others in order for me to establish a reputation as a "tough guy" and a good fighter. I would initiate verbal confrontations and pick fights frequently to bolster the tough guy image I wanted to establish in the African American community. I would even expand my violent exploits to the different sides of town and in the city in an effort to broaden my reputation.

In truth, I really feared a serious challenge to physically defend myself against someone more reputable and physically superior. I wanted to be perceived by my peers as a tough guy. Actually, I did not want my tough guy image to be seriously challenged by a more formidable foe. I abhorred defeat. I feared that a serious loss in a fight would open the floodgates to regular beat downs. A variety of individuals resented my transgressions against others, and harbored long-held revenges against me.

Though seemingly contradictory, my other weaknesses were my love for people in general and my desire to win people's affections at the risk of getting my feelings or person hurt. I realize that this statement seems to contradict my earlier admissions of violent inclinations against others. However, those violent inclinations as I recall, were products of a façade to hide the fears and weaknesses in me that I did not want others to see. In essence the violent inclinations I displayed were not genuine or from the heart, but were a means to an end, a means of survival in a harsh and cruel environment.

One example of my true love for people and willingness to sacrifice myself for others arose when Michael Henry Taylor, one of my Clifton Street gang members and a close childhood friend, and I were traveling home from high school one day on a city bus. On the bus, Michael and I noticed a lone teen stranger being bullied by a small group of high school students about the same age. After witnessing too much bullying, Lil'Mike (as we affectionately called Michael) and I decided to intervene on behalf of the lone teen stranger at the upcoming bus stop. We succeeded, but not without threats from the aggressors that they would deal with us later.

Coincidentally, the aggressors encountered Lil'Mike, a friend Kenny Martin, and I, later that same evening at Watkins Community Center. The aggressors' group, however, had multiplied significantly compared to what it was earlier. They had the community center surrounded with their "troops." Thinking that there was no need for all three of us to be seriously injured or killed, I volunteered to go outside alone and draw the aggressors away from the front door to the side of the building. I decided to absorb whatever retribution they would mete out to me while my friends escaped out the front door to safety. Fortunately, I was only merely beaten up pretty good and that was the end of that episode. Conversely, within the next few weeks, our Clifton Street Gang (a.k.a. Dodge City Territory) cornered several members of the leadership of the original group of aggressors at a party and paid them back in kind. This idea of attack and counter-attack is a prime example of the cycle/psycho of violence and counter-productive behaviors African Americans perpetrate so frequently against each other smack in the heart of our communities.

Our Clifton Street Gang did not qualify as a serious street gang because we did not commit serious crimes or inflict serious injuries or fatalities. Nevertheless, our gang was involved in a number of physical combats with nearby rival neighborhood gangs. We were armed with fists, big sticks, chains, baseball bats, steel pipes, or knives. We were never seriously interested in acquiring firearms, and the introduction of firearms into any of our conflicts was very rare, unless rival gangs used firearms against us.

The only incident that I can recall where a life was taken as a result of our gang activity, was a stupid accident. A wonderful and innocent gentleman named William "Box" Edwards, who was several years our senior, was inadvertently shot through his heart after coming back into Pop's Pool Room located in the 2900 block of North Clifton Street to warn some of us inside that rival gang members were menacingly prowling outside with firearms.

The front door of Pop's Pool Room had no windows and I decided to go to the door and pull it open to peer outside. Box arrived at the door at the same time to leave. I reached the handle of the door first and, as I pulled the door open toward me not realizing the immediate danger on the opposite side, out of courtesy, I allowed Box to step outside in front of me. At the same time, a member of that rival gang was on the opposite side pushing the door open. All three of us were startled by the sudden and unexpected presence of each other and this sparked the assailant to pull the trigger on his gun that released a bullet into Box's chest. Box stumbled forcefully back into my arms, and I immediately got my arms under his armpits and dragged his heels across the floor to safety, in the rear of the pool hall, fearing the shooter would eventually come inside the building and finish us all off. That obviously did not happen, but Box died shortly thereafter. That rival gang was from a community in the Haughville area of Indianapolis and a young man from that group named Emmett Stowers was convicted for the homicide of Box and sentenced to two and up to twenty-one years in prison. He served several years and then was released from prison and enjoyed a number of years of freedom, before his life peacefully expired March 11, 2006. Otherwise, homicides were not a frequent occurrence in Indianapolis at that time.

By now it is obvious that I had joined two gang-like groups almost simultaneously; one in school and the other in the streets that included a few students from the school group. Both groups engaged in petty mischief and juvenile delinquencies. However, the street gang went a step further by committing petty crimes like helping themselves to cakes, pies, and other pastries from Hostess delivery trucks, taking sodas, beer, and other drinks from delivery trucks without proper authorization. The street gang would also vandalize business, city, and private properties; burglarize cars and garages, and steal cars and other property.

One thing is certain: a person cannot seriously be part of a street gang or be a gangster or a thug without being violent. It has been well established that violence is an inherent product of the gangster mentality. As I unequivocally stated in the previous chapter, I have never known or heard of a gang member, gangster, or thug who embraced the principle of "non-violence" as advocated and espoused by Mohandas Gandhi and the Reverend Dr. Martin Luther King, Jr. I would probably give my right arm just to witness first-hand someone being "blessed" into a gang successfully while being allowed to commit to nonviolence. That will never take place. It would probably garner more than a few laughs if it did.

Just as violence is an inherent product of the gangster mentality, so hate is an inherent product of violence. Hate is the most influential emotion that drives people to commit violence against another person, especially murder. So to be violent the person must first be a hater. Most people today are quick to call another person "a hater" or "a player hater." A player hater is one who is jealous or envious of another person's abilities, possessions, or appearance. But if we carefully examined the unkind remarks we have made to and about other people, then we would surely realize the violence and hatred contained in those comments. Hatred can easily produce other negative and damaging feelings: jealousy, disdain, hostility, and animosity toward another person or a thing. These are some of the factors of hate that drive people to commit violent acts against others. In fact, adversaries and enemies are created on the principle of hate. Gangs have adversaries that they compete with or feud with. In essence, to be a gang member, a gangster, a thug, or simply a violent person is to be "a hater."

Most normal human beings are equipped with a conscience, and will resist doing violence to another if there is no credible justification, such as self-defense. But hate itself is generally rooted in some perceived notion of justification. For example, "I hate this person because he or she was selected to a professional sports team and I was not," or "That person thinks I should extend some special respect to her just because she's my employer," or "That snob thinks she's fine because she won the Miss Universe Pageant." But such perceived justification does not make hatred or violence right. A peaceful resolution is always better. A typical gang member is often lured away from the conscientious portion of our society and may originally have been a pleasant human being. But due to some extraneous circumstances, he or she is lured into a deviant association that sends one's life spiraling out of control.

The thing that most aggressors fail to take into account before committing violence against others is the peripheral effects violence has on the people connected to the victim, especially in a case of homicide. The children are deeply affected by the tragic loss of a mother or father; the parents and grandparents are deeply affected by the loss of a son or daughter or grandchild; siblings are deeply affected by the loss of a brother or sister; and friends are deeply affected by the loss of a friend. The death of one victim deeply affects members of the immediate family and sometimes hundreds of others who may be directly or indirectly related to that family. Thousands of other people could also be adversely affected if the victim happened to be a national celebrity or extremely popular. The perpetrator does not kill merely the victim, but also the spirit of many who are adversely affected by the victim's untimely demise. By committing a single homicide, the perpetrator ultimately becomes a serial killer in essence since so many other human beings are killed emotionally and spiritually as a result of the heinous act.

At this point, I add the word *violence* inside the large circle just below the word *thug*. Then I prepare to discuss matters related to the streets, tobacco, alcohol, and drugs.

Low Self-Esteem
Illiteracy

Gang

Thug Life

Violence

Chapter 9

The Streets, Tobacco, Alcohol, and Drugs

A violent reputation is sufficient cause for schools, businesses, churches, synagogues, temples and mosques to severely sanction an individual or even bar him or her from their premises. An institution that tolerates significant violence within its range of authority from those under its supervision creates a counter-productive learning environment and possibly destroys the good reputation and credibility of the institution. This may have an adverse effect on its financial viability. The violent reputation of an individual can also damage his or her family.

Being that I had developed a violent reputation because of many fights with students at school and violent confrontations with rival gangs in the streets, I sensed my trouble-making presence was not welcome in school or my parents' church. That situation ultimately caused tension for me in my parents' home, and I began to spend more and more time in the streets.

The streets became my refuge. I was free from the stress of competing at school both academically and socially. I got the chance to get a break from the rules established by the home, church and school. The streets gave me the freedom to pursue its culturally acceptable activities. The streets practically afforded me autonomy that allowed me to establish my own personal code of conduct. For instance, if I wanted to stand on the street corner and lean against the wall of a sturdy building all day, doing absolutely nothing productive with my time or life, then that is what I did. I did not have to be responsible or accountable for anything or to anyone. It was total freedom to do absolutely nothing and be nothing. In truth, it was actually a worse prison for me than school had been, but I was not intelligent enough at that time to see the situation in those terms. School was much better.

I just did not want to follow rules established by others, especially those like teachers and parents who exerted considerable control and authority over my life. Nevertheless, I was not blatantly disrespectful towards adults and authorities. I was disrespectful in a subtle way, because I would only pretend to be cooperative in the face of adults and authorities but then would covertly break rules and neglect to follow certain instructions issued by them. I would selectively follow the rules and instructions that met my personal objectives whether my objectives were constructive or devious. I made my own rules even though I often subjected myself to severe consequences like days of restriction from leaving home except for school or church. I received suspensions from school in addition to some form of corporal punishments issued by my parents. But this only hardened me more and increased my boldness. My resilient attitude produced from repeated suspensions and punishments solidified the tough guy image that I desired to project and that primarily influenced my decision to integrate deeply into the life of the streets.

I was only trying to fit into an environment that seemed full of people, who enjoyed the freedom to do whatever they chose, whether it involved vegetating on street corners or wearing their hair and clothing in radical styles.

Some of those characters would openly smoke cigarettes, drink alcoholic beverages from bottles, and indiscreetly use illicit drugs. I had already adopted the self-destructive behavior of frequently vegetating on street corners. I began wearing my hair (artificially straightened) and the few clothes I possessed in radical styles. Smoking cigarettes soon followed. I have already discussed earlier in this book the fascination I had with artificially straightening my hair. Now, I will address the issue of cigarette smoking and the issues of drinking alcoholic beverages and using illicit drugs.

This chapter is not designed to help the reader understand the destructive nature of street life, tobacco, alcohol, and drugs, but to increase awareness of how low self-esteem, illiteracy, gang affiliation, the thug and violent mentality which accompanies them can evolve into an increasingly self-destructive cycle of negative and counter-productive activities. I will merely attempt to establish the insanity in the latter four counter-productive activities for purposes of magnified effects, which should not be difficult to achieve for readers with a sound mind.

While a person can acquire many survival skills and a wealth of shrewd experiences from much time spent in the streets, he loses far more than he gains. The streets offer much disappointment, despair, and tragedy, and too many dead end roads. Dreams of escaping from abject poverty or domestic abuse through professed friends in the streets nearly always end in disappointment. This happens often because the person trying to escape does not realize that these so-called friends' agendas may actually be working against him or her. The result of that emotional investment usually produces deeper despair and increases his or her desperation, often leading to criminal activities or other "get rich quick" schemes. The reward for such desperate measures is generally an extensive prison sentence or premature death--thereby the "tragedy" and the "dead end road."

Disappointed dreams of escape from poverty and trouble are often accompanied by other equally unhealthy pursuits. Most people are already aware that tobacco smoking is bad for one's health and even for the non-smoker exposed to second-hand smoke. Look at all the intelligent adults in the world who know the deadly effects of tobacco smoking and chewing. Yet they continue to use this poisonous product. There are updated medical reports, which attest to the adverse effects. These reports flood the media daily. Tobacco consumption is universally understood to be poisonous and more so among heavy smokers. In fact, I understand that tobacco contains at least forty-one different poisons. Surely, most people today know about the enormous amount of poisons in tobacco due to media saturation and the national effort to discourage people from smoking. The use of tobacco products causes all kinds of health problems, such as lung, throat, and mouth cancers. Tobacco use is also known to cause heart disease, strokes, and emphysema. So if a reasonably intelligent human being knows in advance the deadly effects of tobacco use and begins consuming tobacco products, then I would submit that this person is foolish.

I am not sure whether I was aware of the deadly effects of tobacco use during the 1960s when I started smoking at age twelve or thirteen. But I was aware that smoking at that age was socially unacceptable like a lot of the other activities I engaged in at that time. I am a little ashamed to admit this but I probably experimented with tobacco products, booze, and illegal drugs because of a subconscious desire to impress my peers with some level of maturity and to seek approval from my gang members. I believe that many people who are involved with a street-oriented peer group or gang, especially the youth, are influenced to use tobacco, booze, and illegal drugs to seek approval from their peers and to "fit in" to some social network where the use of these products are encouraged.

The purchase and use of tobacco and alcoholic beverages are legal in America, for adults. Though alcoholic beverages are legal for adults, is it not a fact that alcoholic beverages contain both addictive and poisonous ingredients that have effects similar to tobacco on humans? Alcoholic beverages can be just as deadly if consumed in significant quantity and frequency. The addictive agents contained in alcoholic beverages eventually usurp control of the drinker's will, and then the drinker is no longer able to determine when, where, or how much to drink. It is not strange that many products we ingest every day--from tobacco to alcoholic beverages, soft drinks to coffee and chocolate--contain addictive ingredients. In fact, products that include addictive ingredients and are ingested by humans are sometimes, maybe often, an intentional act.

There is undisputed evidence in the past that cigarette manufacturer regularly manipulated levels of nicotine to make their cigarettes more addictive. But is there similar evidence about coffee, chocolate, or even alcohol? Those products are what they are, and the people who make whiskey (or coffee or chocolate) do not manipulate things to make the whiskey (or coffee or chocolate) more powerfully addictive.

Anyone who has prior knowledge of the addictive effects of products such as alcoholic beverages and willingly uses such products habitually at the risk of addiction and demoralizing his or her self is foolishly behaving in a psychopathic manner. I am sure that I was not aware of all the damage caused by long-term use of alcohol, but I was aware of it causing delirium tremens (D.T.'s) because my brother Phillip "Buck" Tinnin suffered from it in my parents' home when I was a small child.

I watched my mother nursing my brother Buck back to health, as he acted delusional and confused about who he is and where he was. Buck appeared to be trying to tie an invisible string from one side of the living room to the other side. I asked my mother, "What's wrong with Buck?" She replied that Buck was suffering from D.T.'s. Then I asked, "What is D.T.'s? She explained that, "it is the withdrawal symptoms a person suffers from being addicted to alcoholic beverages. It is the process of trying to kick the habit." Consequently, I reasoned to myself that I would never have a serious interest in drinking alcoholic beverages, at least regularly. I did, however, have an interest in at least experimenting with them just to see what they tasted like and to see why my father would make all those ugly faces as he swallowed gulps from his Grand Dad bottle. So a short time later while hanging out on the corners socializing with some of my so-called gang buddies, someone in the group persuaded an adult stranger to go into the liquor store to purchase some wine for us. I experimented with wine a few times and something a little stronger a few times as well, but the substance tasted too nasty for me and others tasted even worse. Plus I had a few bad experiences as a result of the drinking.

During one of my few drinking experiences, several of my gang-banging buddies and I were sharing some Wild Irish Rose on the corners of Clifton and Udell Streets, and I quickly got drunk. Suddenly one of the guys, Thomas Phillip "Fat Phil" Johnson, who had been drinking with us, began smacking me in the face while claiming he was trying to smack the drunken stupor out of me. Another person, Herman Louis Barnett, who had also been drinking with us, vehemently ordered Fat Phil to stop. Herman thought it unnecessary for Fat Phil to keep smacking me. When Fat Phil persisted, Herman stabbed him, however, not too seriously, with a medium-sized knife, purportedly in defense of me. Both of those guys were members of our so-called Clifton Street Gang, but such behavior is hardly a sign of camaraderie.

About four or five years later, at the age of 19, I became the target of Herman's aggression. By this time in my life, I had begun the process of becoming a heroin addict. One Friday evening two other gang-banging buddies, the sister of one of them, and I arrived at a party in a car. Jesse "LT" McElwain, Lois "Buddy" McElwain, and Sidney Cox were also in the car. L.T. and Buddy are siblings and Sidney was Buddy's boyfriend. Secretly, I too had a crush on Buddy. As the four of us exited the car to go into the party, we heard a loud familiar voice aggressively and belligerently telling Sidney not to start any trouble at this party. The familiar voice was Herman's. To be fair, Sidney did have a reputation for starting trouble. At that time, I had already exited the car to attend to my extremely urgent need to release some of the fluid from my bladder. I was standing near the car urinating before going into the party. It was very quiet after Herman spoke, and I found it strange that Sidney had not directed any verbal response to Herman since Sidney had always flaunted a tough guy reputation.

Unwilling to allow Herman to get away with "*punk'n*" anybody in our entourage, I decided to respond indirectly to let Sidney know that he would not be alone if he decided to deal with Herman physically. It was an unspoken understanding that none in our entourage could single-handedly defeat Herman in hand-to-hand combat. So I yelled, "Sidney! Tell Herman to kiss your ass." I was still relieving myself when Herman replied, "See, Steve, I was not talking to you," and I quickly retorted, "You can suck my dick." Suddenly and without warning I felt a powerful blow from a fist on my left jaw. I was struck so hard that the blow caused me to spin in a complete circle. I was semi-unconscious but still on my feet and instinctively grabbed my attacker in a bear hug hoping to regain my consciousness and effectively defend myself before Herman dominated me physically. Unfortunately, I was not able to control Herman's aggression. I was not able to compose myself so I could mount an effective defense. Herman went under my legs and through my crotch with his strong hands and upper body strength, raised my body up over his head, and slammed my face and body hard into the concrete sidewalk. I had still been semi-conscious before my body hit the sidewalk. However, after contact with the ground, I was knocked completely out. But Herman still was not through venting his anger and brutal violence on me. As I lay face-down on the sidewalk, unconscious, he began to stomp on the back of my head, forcing my face harder into the concrete while my entourage simply watched without lifting a finger.

Months later someone told me that one of my former grade school classmates, Lonnie Belmar, was at the party and came outside to intervene and pulled Herman away, preventing him from killing me. I truly owe Lonnie a wealth of gratitude and honor for being courageous enough to challenge Herman's vicious assault upon me. Many other party-goers, including two of my so-called gang brothers, stood as spectators and watched as Herman mercilessly stomped me into oblivion. However, Lonnie, with the exception of the females out there, was the only person there humane enough to intervene. I probably would be dead today from that brutal stomping if it were not for his brave undertaking.

That situation permanently marred my association with gangs and my confidence in individuals who are gang members. It deeply disappointed me to realize that most guys in our so-called gang were not really hardcore and brave. Instead, they proved that many of them have only group-courage and when separated from the group their abundant weaknesses are exposed. I reasoned that most guys who migrate to gang membership are actually cowards who fear traveling through life on their own merits and ultimately cannot be trusted to protect the back of their partners. My new attitude towards gangs and gang members influenced my decision to pursue life acting solo. I also reasoned that a real man stands on his own merits and does not need another man or a group of men to validate his manhood just as a real woman does not need other women to validate her womanhood.

After that beating, and Lonnie's intervention, I was rushed to the hospital where another dramatic story developed in relation to that brutal beating. I regained consciousness in the hospital a few hours later. I was alone with the exception of hospital personnel and an Indianapolis Police Department officer assigned to the hospital that night. None of my so-called friends or gang-banging buddies was at the hospital with me. I was, however, still mildly semi-unconscious when I woke up. I noticed immediately that my left jaw was swollen like a melon. I learned later that my jaw was fractured. Both of my lips were uncommonly swollen and split in the center, requiring several stitches in each lip. Too upset, angry, and vindictive to hang around the hospital to receive medical treatment, I immediately attempted to leave. However, the police officer would not allow me to leave. He determined that I needed medical treatment badly. He no doubt also suspected I wanted to leave the hospital prematurely to mete out vengeance on whoever was responsible for my injuries. He was right.

I repeatedly warned the officer to get out of my way and told him he could not make me receive medical treatment if I did not want it. He insisted. I reasoned that it was useless to try and persuade this police officer to allow me to leave the hospital. I began to measure the officer in my mind, assessing whether I could knock him out with a powerful blow before he was able to grab his gun. I would then be able to leave the hospital without further delay. So I hit the officer in the face, knocking him to the floor, and then attempted to flee the hospital, but to no avail. The nurses and doctors instantly converged on me like a team of defensive football players and collectively placed me on a gurney and firmly tied all four of my limbs to it. The police officer eventually got up off the floor and placed me under arrest for assault on a police officer after he punched me in my already injured mouth.

Upon my arrival at the jail, the jailers were immediately notified that I was the person who assaulted the police officer at the hospital, and the jailers instantly left their work stations and physically attacked me. The police carried out this brutal and illegal retribution on me periodically on each shift during the entire weekend. I will always remember December 12, 1969, as one of my most awful days because of the awful beating I incurred at the hands of Herman Louis Barnett and the multiple beatings I suffered later at the hands of the Indianapolis Police Department. I appeared in court the following Monday morning and received a prison sentence of 180 days on the Indiana State Farm (currently Putnamville Correctional Facility) for Assault & Battery and for Resisting Arrest.

The police officer that I assaulted, Warren Edward Greene, eventually was killed in the line of duty on December 20, 1975, while investigating a domestic disturbance. I discovered sometime in 2001 that he was the father of my current good friend and supervisor Melvin Greene. Melvin Green worked as the Director of Transition Programs for the Indiana Department of Correction.

The irony of this whole situation is that the male assailant who killed Officer Greene lived near the corner of 26th Street and Boulevard Place where the homicide occurred. I lived approximately three blocks away at 2940 Boulevard Place with Karen Marie Grundy, the mother of my three daughters Stephanie, Cassandra, and Joycelyn. It is also ironic that the assailant and I were casual friends and met at a bus stop at 26th and Northwestern Avenue (currently Dr. Martin Luther King Street) every weekday morning to ride the bus to school where we attended a G.E.D. program (which I failed to complete at that time) for adults. The class was located behind the Lockfield

Gardens near General Hospital (currently Wishard Memorial Hospital). The assailant would occasionally talk to me about his suspicion that his uncle was having an affair with his girlfriend. I cannot recall the assailant's name, but he ultimately killed himself after he killed his uncle and the first police officer who arrived on the scene, Officer Warren Greene. I was able to visit the scene of the crime because it occurred just before the assailant and I were to catch the bus for school that morning and it happened along the route I walked to the bus stop each week day morning.

The cumulative circumstances that involve Mel Greene, his late father, and me, add credence to the old adage that "This is a small world." Mel is the person who influenced IDOC officials to offer me contract employment in the year 2000 and who has mentored me since that time and made other constructive contributions that ultimately enabled me to enjoy a better quality of life. Mel is obviously another great person I owe a substantial amount of gratitude.

So after the unfortunate stabbing incident that I believed did not warrant such a drastic response, I realized that I was opposed to ever getting drunk again. I quit drinking alcoholic beverages as quickly as I had started. At that same time, a number of my young friends, and other young people throughout the economically depressed neighborhoods of Indianapolis who were addicted to drinking cheap wines and other liquors developed the notorious disease cirrhosis of the liver, or kidney disease. They also suffered strokes and subsequently died a short time later. Nevertheless, I was under the impression then that "getting high" off some man-made product was as common for Americans as apple pie. On the other hand, since drinking liquor did not work out for me, I set out to discover something else that would satisfy my lust for "getting high."

Steven "Oz" Osborn, another member in our so-called Clifton Street Gang who was a few years older, invited me to take a few drags off his marijuana cigarette and coached me on the proper way to smoke it. I had smelled this stuff several times in the past at different locations in the neighborhood, but I had never smoked any until Oz gave me some on this particular occasion. I seldom desired to smoke "weed" because I did not like the way it affected me.

Reports from the media claims, "that marijuana use can damage a person's health as seriously as cigarettes do, or worse. In fact, marijuana is as addictive as cigarettes are." But what really disturbs me is, despite all the modern medical reports to the contrary, the many purported justifications that so-called intelligent and upstanding people use to justify their continued use of marijuana. I have even heard some people claim that marijuana is not a drug or dope but I would reply, "Then, go to the police station and smoke some in the midst of some police officers and see what happens to you." Others claim that marijuana is okay because it is a plant that God created, and I would reply, "God also created the coca, which is a tropical shrub or plant whose dried leaves are the source of cocaine, and God created the poppy, which is a plant as well whose deeply cut leaves are the source of opium and heroin." A published report on the "Negative Effects of Marijuana" produced by Kathy Gable that I retrieved from the internet states that,

> "Marijuana is a drug made from the cannabis plant. THC is the most potent active chemical in marijuana, and it is THC that produces the negative effects of marijuana use. When you smoke marijuana, THC enters the blood stream through the lungs and is pumped throughout the body to your brain and vital organs. THC then interacts with certain areas of the brain to produce the high that is associated with using marijuana.

The area of the brain impaired by marijuana controls pleasures, sensory function, physical coordination, memory and relationship to time. This means that when you smoke marijuana, senses are dulled, physical abilities are impaired, and coherency and ability to think clearly is reduced. The length of these impairments depends on the amount of marijuana that has been smoked or otherwise ingested into the body and at what frequency.

Marijuana is typically smoked, providing the same negative effects to the body as smoking other substances. It contains many carcinogens that damage lung tissue and may lead to cancer. Marijuana use also raises your heart rate and blood pressure, leading to an increased risk of heart attack.

Marijuana is a highly addictive drug. Addiction to marijuana can develop rapidly and make it difficult to stop using the drug, even when a person wants to do so. This addiction impairs ability to function normally in school, social, and work setting. It is difficult to hide an addiction to marijuana as many workplaces require urine tests from their employees to screen for presence of the drug, making it difficult for those using the drug to find employment and stay employed.

Deterioration of mental health is a secondary but important effect of marijuana addiction. Marijuana addicts experience increased irritability, depression and inability to maintain healthy relationships. This impact on mental health, impacts all areas of life, which means the overall quality of life for marijuana users is decreased.

While still disputed, many feel that marijuana is a primary gateway drug. This means that marijuana use is often a stepping stone to the abuse of other more serious illegal drugs. Even though this has not been firmly proven, the risk is significant enough to consider when contemplating the negative effects of marijuana use."

I can attest to the truth of a substantial portion of what Kathy Gable states above as a result of my marijuana use briefly as a teenager and then a little more extensively later as an adult. Though I never became addicted to marijuana in a technical sense, it did hamper my ability to think clearly and function normally in school and in other social settings. In fact, it caused me to behave childishly and ultimately influenced my decision to use more serious illegal drugs, such as heroin and cocaine.

Marijuana would cause me to laugh endlessly and uncontrollably about anything as minor as how someone walked or talked. So after smoking "weed" several times over several months, I stopped smoking it and began using illicit pills called "Blue Tips" and "Red Devils." These were sold on the streets and ingested orally. My use of these illicit pills lasted only a few months. The pills would occasionally cause my friends and I to passed out for a couple of days or discover ourselves locked up in the juvenile detention center the following morning. Since I was not aware of the magnitude of my pursuit of "getting high" at that time, I persisted to travel down the road of self-destruction in search of my drug of choice. Many other people are guilty of the same pursuits, and this behavior is definitely a symptom of insanity.

But how many of us really acknowledge that some of our behavior is insane? Helping people to realize this insanity is the intent of this book; I hope this book functions as a mirror that reflects some of our deviant behaviors, which we are normally oblivious to or simply in denial.

I have discussed the adverse effects of street life, tobacco, and alcoholic beverages on human beings. Obviously, I did not provide information here that even the simple reader would not already know. This information should merely function as a reminder for everyone. The mind never forgets, but it may fail to recall certain things at times. To combat this forgetfulness, I will provide some reminders here about the effects of drugs. First, drugs are, of course, useful when people are ill or suffering from some disease and a licensed physician legally prescribes drugs to heal or relieve the patient's suffering. In that case, the patient consumes the drugs as prescribed by the doctor. The legal and legitimate use of drugs is not my subject here, however. There is nothing wrong or insane about using medical resources in the right way. I am about to discuss the use of illicit drugs.

After I realized, at the age 19, that alcohol and illicit pills did not satisfy my desire to get high, I began to experiment with injecting heroin into my veins. Within a few days, I became addicted to this narcotic. Because I liked the way it made me feel, I used the extremely addictive drug several days in succession. It took only a short time for me to realize that I had gotten in way over my head by meddling with heroin. Its intensely addictive ingredients clutched me in a powerful grip so that my only permanent escape would be to enter prison. I was aware of information floating through "the grapevine" that heroin and cocaine are highly addictive narcotics. I was simply deluded about heroin and cocaine's addictive powers, both physical and psychological. I reasoned that since I was able to walk away *cold-turkey* from the addictive influences of alcoholic beverages and the previous use of marijuana, I could walk away from anything I desired. While I may have vaguely understood the physical addictions of heroin and cocaine prior to using heroin, I obviously failed to understand their psychological effects. Several times, I refrained from using heroin for five or six days after going through several days of excruciating physical withdrawals, but I would eventually return to its use because I had not overcome my psychological addiction to the drug. Time after time, I stopped using heroin for days, weeks, and, on one occasion, for several years, but I eventually relapsed because I had not accounted for the power of its psychological addiction.

Heroin use and abuse have been responsible for numerous health problems incurred by hundreds of my friends and associates. Its use can cause heart attack, cardiac arrest, and aneurysm as well as lung, kidney, and liver diseases plus various sexually transmitted diseases via sharing intravenous needles. Most importantly, though, I witnessed a number of my friends' and associates' health slowly deteriorates physically to the point where they looked like skeletons with only skin on their bones. They died a very short time later. And many of my friends and associates died prematurely from a drug overdose.

Addiction to vices such as tobacco, alcoholic beverages, drugs, profanity, gambling, and sex equates to a list of weaknesses. The dictionary defines "vice" as:

1. a. An evil, degrading, or immoral practice or habit. b. A serious moral failing.

2. Wicked or evil conduct or habits; corruption.

3. Sexual immorality, especially prostitution.

4. A slight personal failing; foible.

5. A flaw or imperfection; defect.

6. A physical defect or weakness.

Usually a human being wants others to perceive him or her as a strong individual in stature, image, and character. No normal person desires to be perceived by others as a weakling because of the likelihood of becoming an instant target of someone's aggression, whether it is harassment, assault, theft, or some other serious offense. Ultimately, how can a person honestly project a strong image or character when he or she has a number of vices, thus weaknesses? Some of the most intelligent and athletic people in our society smoke tobacco, operate motor vehicles drunk, use drugs, and spew loud profanities in public. Some community leaders, education administrators, teachers, radio and television personalities, fire and police officials, lawyers and judges, legislators and presidents of the United States appear strong and pious in the public and speak with clarity and confidence until their indiscretions (vices) are exposed. Consider, for example, a report in the *Indianapolis Star* on September 28, 2009, entitled "Former Indiana Priest Apologizes for Actions:

> A former Catholic priest who served in Indiana and stands accused in more than 20 lawsuits of molesting altar boys is apologizing for his actions.
>
> In an interview with the Burlington (Vt.) Free Press at his home in Westfield, Mass., 80-year-old Edward Paquette said he prays daily for the families of the people he harmed.
>
> According to court documents, Paquette molested boys from the 1950s through the 1970s at parishes in Massachusetts, Indiana and Vermont.

Furthermore, it is common knowledge that the late Richard Nixon was pressured to resign from the office of President of the United States due to his criminal indiscretions. Also, former President Bill Clinton was subjected to impeachment proceedings for some sexual indiscretions, and that Washington, D.C., Mayor Marion Berry was convicted while in office for possessing and using crack cocaine. Of course, I could name hundreds more prominent personalities who have incurred public disgrace for crimes or indiscretions, but I am sure I have made my point. In all these situations, the world suddenly witnesses the previously strong, pious, and confident character disintegrating almost instantly into embarrassment. The weaknesses of the individual have therefore been exposed, and the proof of any human's fallibility is manifested. We become strong by successfully resisting indulgence in destructive or counter-productive activities, products, and people. This is not to say that a person cannot be redeemed after committing indiscretions and ultimately be restored to a level of dignity such as the case of former President Bill Clinton, who is widely respected for what he has done since his presidency ended. A person's dignity and credibility can be restored once the person has demonstrated sufficient contrition in the eyes of the public as President Clinton tries earnestly to achieve with his humanitarian acts around the world.

Finally, despite all the other people, issues and circumstances I included in this chapter, my primary intent here has been to demonstrate how and why my psychopathic personality evolved from one deviant characteristic in succession to others. These include low self-esteem, illiteracy, gang involvement, thug life attitudes, the practice of violence, engaging in the life on the streets, using tobacco, alcoholic beverages, and illegal drugs. In upcoming chapters, developments that are more deviant will be revealed.

Another factor I shall not fail to discuss is the issue of financially maintaining tobacco, alcohol, and drug addictions once these addictions are acquired. I will take up this issue in the next chapter. Right now, though, I will write inside the large circle the words "Streets," "Tobacco," "Alcohol," and "Drugs" in clockwise order, respectively.

Low Self-Esteem

Illiteracy

Gang

Thug Life

Violence

Streets

Tobacco

Alcohol

Drugs

Chapter 10

Unemployment, Hustling, and Materialism

U nemployment was no big deal for me early in life because laziness and lack of motivation caused allergic reactions in my confused mind whenever someone ordered or suggested I do some form of manual labor.

Once I had become accustomed to smoking an occasional cigarette at the age of thirteen and learned that I would not continue to get them free, I had to consider other ways to procure cigarettes. I had no money except for the small change my mother sometimes left in her purse unattended on top of her dresser. I needed to find some means to generate income. I thought about cutting grass for people who lived in our community so I could earn a few dollars. I even thought about approaching the owner of a mom and pop store in the community to do odd jobs around the store. I did not have any formal skills to do anything else in a store. All the stores in the community, however, already had little helpers like me. As a result, I considered just going to a typical business nearby and fill out a formal application. I quickly realized, however, not only that I really was not old enough for a job designed for young adults or older, but also that I was not literate enough to fill out the application without someone's help. So I remained unemployed until months later when my father had me to accompany him every Saturday, from 10:00 a.m. until 6:00

p.m., to the home of an elderly widow, Mrs. Adams, to do yard and household work.

Mrs. Adams was a wealthy Caucasian woman who had been married many years to, I believe, a retired military colonel. She lived on the north side of Indianapolis on the corner of 56th and N. Delaware Streets. Mrs. Adams was a very pleasant and kind lady. She also employed my grandmother and one of my father's sisters. My father provided my very first instructions on how to artistically cut the grass on a lawn and how to professionally manicure the lawn during this one-day-a-week job. Pop also taught me how to maintain Mrs. Adams's huge basement, shovel the snow off her sidewalks and driveway, and effectively nourish the numerous plants in her greenhouse. Though I missed some Saturdays working with Pop, it was a year-round occupation for a couple of years. I never understood why my father chose me out of his seven sons to accompany him on Saturdays to work. Maybe he chose me because I was born in the center, three brothers older and three younger. Also, my eldest brother Dickie had relocated to California at that time. My second eldest brother Buck was always preoccupied with the effects of cheap wine, and my third eldest brother Curtis was busy producing babies and arranging his repeated marriages. Much later in life I figured that he chose me probably because he had envisioned me traveling down a future path of self-destruction and wanted to keep me near him as much as possible to protect me from myself.

Mrs. Adams paid my father an undisclosed amount at the end of the long day. My father then paid me an average of twelve dollars. Today twelve dollars may not seem like much money for an eight-hour day of work, but that work was classified as menial. Besides, it was the early 1960s when a pack of cigarettes cost only thirty-five cents. In fact, that was the last meaningful employment I would have for at least the next eleven years.

I worked with my father for twelve dollars on Saturdays from the age of thirteen until I was fifteen. Twelve dollars was quite a bit of money for youth in depressed communities, still I needed to generate supplemental income to compensate for those Saturdays I did not work. Also, for new needs I gradually developed such as buying more expensive and stylish apparel, shoes, and attending teen functions. Having a Saturday-only job really did not suffice, so as a result I considered ways of doing some on-the-side hustling to acquire extra money. I was not the only person in my peer group/street gang that hung out on street corners who believed hustling was a good way to get some money. A few of us walked through the neighborhoods periodically together armed with lawn mowers, rakes, and shovels and offered our yard services to anyone willing to pay us. We did not make much money because many people in the neighborhoods found it less expensive to care for their own properties. But whatever money we made we split evenly. Due to society's glamorizing of material wealth and fashion, gang members in our group soon learned that we did not earn enough money to buy most of what we desired.

The desire to acquire certain material and fashionable items rapidly, preoccupied the mind, for many in our so-called gang. Having popular material items like Converse gym shoes, Stacy Adams dress shoes, leather jackets, and various jeans and dress pants gave us a sense of individual importance, prominence, and power in the community. Though imaginary, I am sure it gave us a sense of celebrity status, in the community and created influence for us over others. We obviously valued this status very much and at times extremely because it caused us to feel good about ourselves. In addition to maintaining that status, we resorted to drastic measures, even violence. Like most of the people in America, we had become materialistic in our views. The dictionary definitions of *materialism* relevant to this discussion are as follows:

materialism- n.   2.   The theory or doctrine that physical well-being and worldly possessions constitute the greatest good and highest value in life.

3 A great or excessive regard for worldly concerns.

Consequently, a materialistic person places more value on worldly possession. They are preoccupied with status or reputation and are inconsiderate of human lives. The materialistic person can potentially be very dangerous, lashing out vindictively or violently against anyone who apparently devalues something highly valued by the materialistic person. For example, when a gang member encounters a member of a rival gang wearing opposing colors or symbols, they both become hostile toward one another, disregarding the value of another human being. In fact, they may not know one another. However, because the color each of them wears and the corresponding symbols each embraces are highly valued, the opposing color and symbols are generally despised.

Gang affiliation colors and symbols become an obsession with many gang members to the point where they would never buy or wear clothing and shoes that reflect the colors of a rival gang. A particular color in and of itself becomes an extremely valued symbol among many gang members whereas this obsession is not only reflected in their fancy dress but also on the paint of their flashy cars. I understand these things because I grew up in this culture plus I continue to interact daily with young people who are gang members. My relationships with barbershops, vendors in the African American community, and my occupational positions in public schools and various Indiana prisons I visit, entrust me with wisdom to understand these kinds of behaviors. The colors and symbols are material things, and a person is considered materialistic who places more value on a color or a thing than on another human being. The same principle applies to someone who places more value on his or her neighborhood or "hood" than on a person's life. They have no qualms about harming another person simply because that person does not live in the neighborhood being defended.

Even though it is not a tangible thing, an individual's reputation can be considered a materialistic thing if the individual places "excessive regard" on his or her reputation since in fact a reputation is a worldly concern. In statement #3 of the definition "materialism" it defines another perspective of materialism as: "A great or excessive regard for worldly concerns." So if a person harms another person in any way simply because one defames the other, then the aggressor can simply be considered a materialistic person as it relates to statement #3 of the definition of materialism.

Their excessive materialism is primarily what alienated me from the "more fortunate" students in school. Now, it appeared that I was experiencing alienation all over again from the very teens I migrated to, in order to feel secure and escape the alienation I experienced in school. Nevertheless, I absorbed this materialistic mentality, to diminish the alienation I was beginning to experience again and began my own pursuit of the material things I imagined would make me popular and thereby less alienated.

I set out to acquire all the fashionable stuff within my power-especially expensive shoes, clothes, and jewelry. Unlike the youth of today who can often afford a car and the accessories that come with it, most teens during my youth, especially in my economically depressed neighborhood, could not afford a car and were satisfied to ride the city bus. Clothes and shoes were our main objects of fascination and vying with one another for popularity.

In addition to purchasing the popular Chuck Taylor Converse gym shoes and keeping a fresh pair on our feet during the 1960s, we were also under peer pressure in the community to maintain a few pairs of Stacy Adams dress shoes, leather coats, and particular name brand shirts and pants. Subsequently, the famous European musical band from England, The Beatles, emerged on the scene and brought along with them their hit songs, Beatle hairstyle, and Beatle boots.

Like most teens and young adults of every race throughout the nation, many of our gang members purchased Beatle records, Beatle boots, and Beatle wigs. A number of us in the group, however, could not afford these items, but the peer pressure to fit in intensified. This kind of peer pressure is what young people today experience in relation to "old school" automobiles and modern fashionable gym shoes and apparel, which they relish and love to own. Some of today's young people even desire to add a number of expensive accessories to their "old school" cars, such as a candy paint job, 24 and 26-inch tires, chrome rims, 18-inch speakers in the trunk accompanied by a sophisticated radio system, and video screens positioned strategically around the interior of the car. Like the young people of my time, young people today want fashionable items and it establishes the individual's importance and prestige. This is the mentality of a materialistic person. These materialistic desires accompanied by a lack of money are the ingredients that induce someone to conjure some deviant means to fulfill those desires.

I return to the board to write the words *unemployment*, *hustling*, and *materialistic* while preparing for the next and final topics for discussion to be placed in the circle.

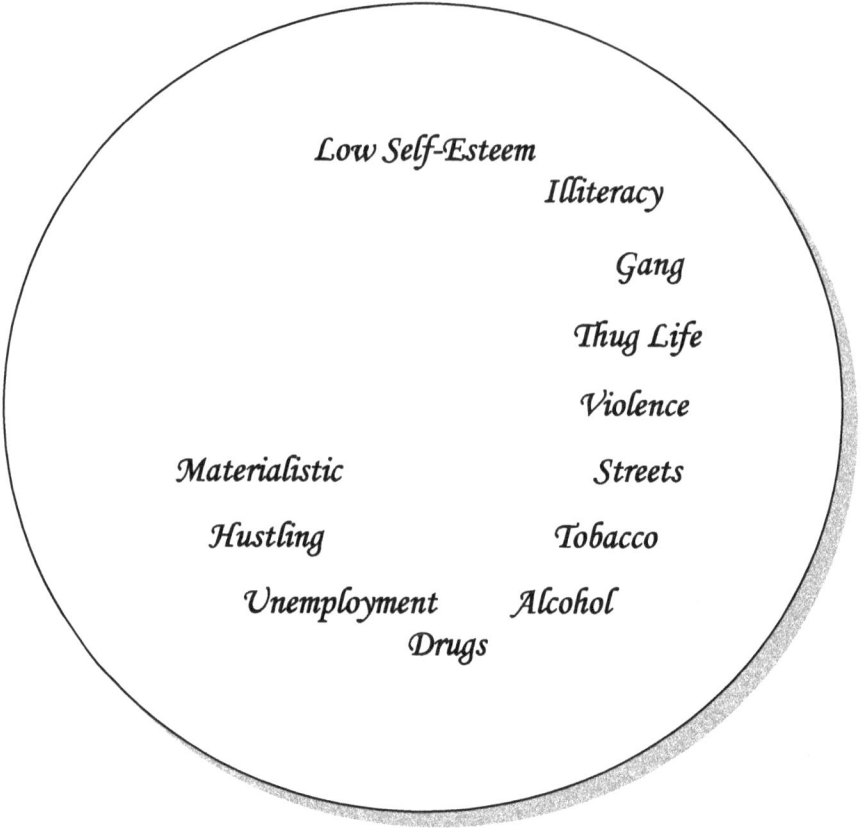

Chapter 11

Crimes, Arrest, Detention, and Release

As young mischievous boys between the ages of twelve and fourteen, a number of us represented the junior portion of the Clifton Street Gang. Some of the mischief we engaged in entailed stealing cupcakes and pies from the Hostess truck while the Hostess driver was inside a store making a delivery. We would also organize clandestine operations among ourselves. We did this to conduct surveillance on other commercial trucks that delivered milk, bread, soda, and beer. We wanted to ascertain their weekly schedules so that we could establish an exact day and time to sneak up to the vehicle to steal some of its cargo partly for the excitement, but also to satisfy our thirst or our sweet tooth. There was no monetary motivation for our attacks on the commercial vehicles except in the sense that we were getting something for nothing. Perhaps, what was most dangerous or damaging about these escapades, was that our success with those deviant acts probably furnished many of us with a sense of intelligence and achievement that we failed to attain in school.

During our deviant acts, we often walk together, four or five of us. We walk through alleys in the neighborhoods stealing fashionable clothes off the clotheslines in certain backyards. Once we felt comfortable about entering strange backyards to steal clothing, we began entering garages to take tools, lawnmowers, and other equipments. The proceeds that came from the stolen items and selling them on the black market, provided many of us sufficient buying power to purchase the more expensive and fashionable items like coats, clothes, and shoes. This made us feel good about ourselves and prominent in our young and foolish segment of our communities.

Our graduation into stealing valuable items, replaced our original motivations of excitement, thirst, and hunger with the more serious motivation of monetary gain. The driving force, behind our criminal pursuits of substantial money during the 1960s and '70s by economically depressed teens and young adults was the need to feel important and to be prominent. These are the very impetuses that drive today's young people to try to achieve wealth through dealing illicit drugs and engaging in other criminal activities.

Dealing illicit drugs in today's black market is incredibly lucrative and is extremely attractive particularly for young people. The accumulation of wealth and abundant material possessions are generally new and exciting adventures for young people whereas older people usually have already enjoyed those experiences and the desire for those things has waned with the passing of time. Dealing illicit drugs potentially produces instant wealth and power for people commonly unaccustomed to neither. Young people are so attracted to this particular criminal activity because it is generally accompanied with something like celebrity status in the "hood." Celebrity status, of course, provides these commonly obscure individuals a sense of importance, at least among their peers.

During the 1960s, we even began to expand our economic horizons by exploring other clandestine endeavors that would create additional economic opportunities for us. In addition to the previously mentioned deviant acts, we eventually developed an interest in stealing dogs of particular breeds. At that time, many people in our economically depressed neighborhoods apparently desired dogs like the German shepherd, Doberman pinscher, and Boxer. People prefer these dogs largely for their intimidating demeanors, for property and personal protection, and for social status; in much the same way, people today flaunt their Pit Bulls. Many people in my old neighborhood would pay a generous dollar on the black market to own such dogs. A few of the younger members of the Clifton Street Gang worked to satisfy that black market for the purchase of stolen dogs at a cut-rate price. Some of the youth who made up this clique of black market dog dealers included Michael "Lil'Mike" Taylor, Kenneth "Crazy Kenny" Martin, James "Dynamite" McDuffy, Richard "Rock" Maul, Eric "Little Dee" Murray, Ronald "Black Ronnie" Hoskins and me. As we traveled the alleys in neighborhoods, a couple of us would lure the adult dogs away from their puppies while others grabbed, if possible, all the puppies. If the adult dogs were friendly enough then we took them as well and used them to produce additional puppies for sale. We became so infamous in our community for stealing and selling dogs that whenever someone wanted to purchase a dog on the black market or discovered their dog or dogs missing, that person would seek us out as black market dog dealers or as culprits in the theft of their dogs.

Members in our clique would, on average, make between $50 and $150 per dog--quite a bit of money during the 1960s in the pockets of youngsters between twelve and fourteen. That money supplemented the comparatively small amount of money I made working with my father at the wealthy elderly lady's home on some Saturdays.

Still, the income I made from the sale of stolen dogs lasted only a short time. Sometime in January 1966, I incurred my first arrest by police and was charged with theft. The theft charge was based on some German shepherd puppies I had stolen. My first interrogation by police detectives was easy for them. The stolen puppies were practically in my possession since in fact they were discovered on my parents' front porch. I was not about to shift suspicion to any other member of my family when I was the only one involved with the theft of dogs. So I readily admitted to detectives that I was the only person responsible for stealing the puppies.

I appeared in juvenile court the following day to answer to the charge of theft of the dogs. After the female juvenile judge informed me that I had been formally charged with the theft of some dogs, she asked, "How do you plead?" I replied, "Guilty." The judge then asked, "Why did you steal the dogs?" I decided that I had better not tell the judge the truth about stealing the dogs to sell them for money. Of course the dogs that I had been charged with stealing were not the only dogs I had stolen. Not only had I stole the dogs I was in court being tried for, but, I had been stealing dogs practically every day for at least 4 years before being caught. I along with my juvenile accomplices probably stole over several hundred adult dogs and puppies and committed a multitude of other minor crimes from stealing candy bars and other sweets out of neighborhood mom and pop stores, to breaking in cars, stealing 8-track stereos and breaking in garages stealing lawnmowers and other equipments. So instead of telling the judge the truth about why I stole the puppies, I told the judge a lie that I imagined would reflect some sort of humanitarian perspective about my character in the eyes of the court, thus hoping to earn me leniency from the judge. I told the lie because I was a bit scared and petrified about the prospect of being locked up in a detention facility no matter if the time was for a brief or extensive period. My response to the judge was that: "I stole the dogs because I love animals." "You love animals uh," the judge replied in a sarcastic manner. As a result, the judge sentenced me to be detained indefinitely in the Marion County Juvenile Detention Center, and to be seen by a psychiatrist twice each week.

I remained in the juvenile detention center for four months and talked with a psychiatrist twice each week. The juvenile center had a voluntary educational system in place for juveniles who desired to continue their education, but during that period in my life, I had an aversion to education. When I was not talking to the psychiatrist as mandated by the court, I played card games, dominoes, checkers, chess, ping-pong, volleyball, and basketball, but I did not spend one minute improving my education. While detained in the center, all I did was play games and had a good time. I cannot recall clearly what the psychiatric treatment entailed, but I can recall that the psychiatrist often handed me pictures with various animals in them. Some of the pictures were, a person standing inside or outside a home, a person and an animal together in some friendly relationship. Then the psychiatrist would require me to write a story about what I envisioned in the pictures. After four months of that psychiatric treatment, I was released from the detention center to my parents.

For the final time I return to the white dry-erase board to write the last three words, *crimes*, *detention*, and *release* inside the large circle, which completes the cycle.

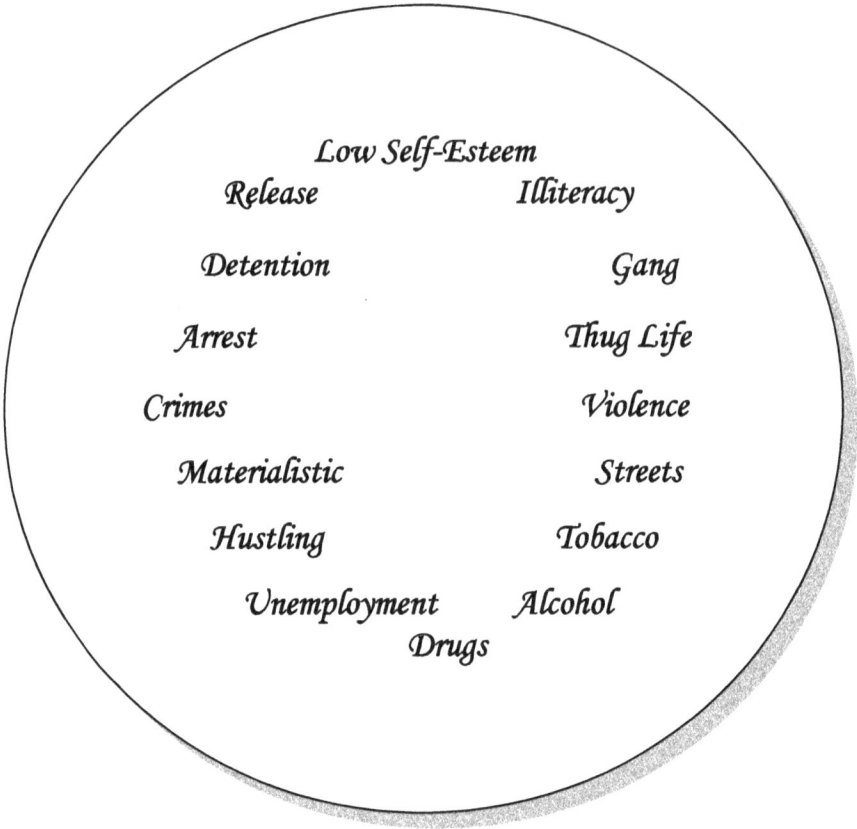

Low Self-Esteem
Release   Illiteracy

Detention   Gang

Arrest   Thug Life

Crimes   Violence

Materialistic   Streets

Hustling   Tobacco

Unemployment   Alcohol
Drugs

Chapter 12

Repeating the Negative
and
Counter-Productive Cycle

This chapter actually presents the essential key to the psychopathic personality. For example, I failed during the period of detention to correct at least my first two character flaws (low self-esteem and illiteracy) that I enumerated in the large circle on the white dry-erase board.

Those first two character flaws in my cycle of negative and counter-productive behaviors also represented the impetus to the succeeding character flaws in my cycle: the gang involvement, the thug mentality, the violence, the life in the streets, the abuse of tobacco, alcohol and drugs, the unemployment, the hustling, the materialism, the crime, the detention, and finally the release. My failure during the period of detention to seize upon the opportunity to obtain meaningful education and eliminate my serious illiteracy indicated not only that I did not love myself, but also that I still suffered from low self-esteem. Upon my release from detention, I was still suffering from low self-esteem and illiteracy. Therefore, I returned unchanged to the very environment where I found some comfort among people who shared similar character flaws, and who I felt at ease with. The downside of this situation, though, was that it influenced in me the propensity to repeat the same negative and counter-productive behaviors, which brought the same or worse consequences.

Ultimately, I did repeat that counter-productive cycle, and the behaviors and crimes grew worse. Returning to the very environment that influenced the bad behaviors that led to my original arrest and detention led me to the same bad behaviors all over again and produced similar consequences as a result. I hung out with the same guys who were now involved in more serious deviant behaviors, and added experiences may have emboldened them. In order for me to keep pace with my peers, I grew bolder.

Between the ages of fourteen to sixteen, I returned a number of times to the juvenile detention for minor crimes such as disorderly conduct, fleeing from law enforcement, assault and battery, petty larceny, and auto theft.

On July 3, 1967, Crazy Kenny, Lil' Mike, Little Dee, and I decided to burglarize an Army and Navy Surplus Store to steal bayonets, swords, and cans of mace to use as weaponry for our gang-banging. We also stole jewelry and other valuables from the business. Since we did not own a vehicle, we had to escape with the stolen items by carrying them in our hands and over our arms. We slipped out of the business with the stolen items after carefully checking the traffic in both directions for police cars and determined the coast was clear. We had to cross West 16th Street where the business was located, from south to north, in order to head toward our homes with the bounty. But as we reached the middle of the street, we saw to our right that one of the cars coming over the Fall Creek Bridge was a police patrol car. Assuming instinctively that the police would recognize right away that we were carrying a bunch of stolen items, we immediately scampered in different directions to elude the police. Unfortunately, for me, the police chose me out of the four of us to pursue. That pursuit lasted only a few moments, because I mistakenly ran in the direction of a fenced-in area and was thus easily cornered. I still attempted to scale the tall fence by grasping it with my hands and taking at least one step toward the top. The police officer, however, had drawn his service weapon and loudly warned me to stop. I did not want to die that day, so I came down off the fence to surrender.

I cooperated when the officer put a handcuff on one of my wrists. However, a short time later, I realized that I was recently released from the juvenile detention center and did not want to return so soon, thus I used my free hand to snatch the officer's firearm from its holster. The officer and I struggled for control of the weapon for a very short time. He was obviously trained expertly in defending himself and subduing suspects. He effectively repelled my aggression and had me secured in both handcuffs in seconds.

The juvenile court expressed frustration with trying to habilitate me, determined that I was apparently incorrigible, and therefore waived me to adult court at the age of fifteen years and eleven months. I was immediately transferred to the Marion County Jail and at a time when juvenile cellblocks and the separation of offenders according to their crimes had not been instituted yet. I was placed therefore in a cellblock with adult males who were charged with a variety of crimes from theft to child molestation, rape, and murder.

Those big heavy steel doors of the cellblocks bang loudly against their steel frames when opening and closing. I thought at the time, could wake the dead. When the deputy sheriffs opened the door to cellblock 3D and ordered me inside, the loud noise from the opening of the door apparently woke up every sleeping inmate in that cellblock because they all seemed to come to attention to observe me entering. I looked straight into each of the faces in range of my vision and saw only unfamiliar faces. None of them showed any sign of recognizing me. I reasoned that the difference between my age and theirs—most in their 20s, 30s, 40s, and 50s-was probably the reason we were not familiar with one another. Shortly thereafter, I realized that a few of the men in there apparently considered me a possible target of their perverted inclinations because they began whistling like men do to communicate inappropriately to women deemed sexy.

I felt disrespected as well as a tremendous sense of emotional discomfort and began preparing myself mentally to defend against any physical aggression that might come to me directly. I was not sure if they were serious, joking, or just testing me. Unexpectedly, one of the men in the cellblock asked, "What's your name?" I replied, "Steve Tinnin." Then another person asked, "Are you any kin to Buck Tinnin?" My anxiety level began to diminish with a sense of relief. Apparently, someone here knew my brother, and that alone, might alleviate my need to defend my manhood. So I quickly responded "yes" and went on to state, "Buck is an older brother of mine." I learned later that the person who asked that question was Richard "Richie" Cooper. Richie and a few other guys indicated that they knew some of my older siblings. Richie and I soon became friends because he exuded a genuine character, a pleasant personality, and used his influence in the cellblock to discourage any aggression against me. Thank God! Everyone in the cellblock admired Richie for his humor and his kind personality and especially his ability to sing almost as well as the renowned crooner Smokey Robinson. Those events in jail occurred in 1967 when there were no televisions or radios allowed in cellblocks. The only music we had in jail then was Richie Cooper and occasionally other inmates who could sing as well.

Months later, I was taken from the jail to appear in court for a bench trial. I had turned 16 while waiting to go to court. I was easily found guilty of 2nd degree burglary and sentenced to an adult penal institution, the Indiana State Farm (currently Putnamville Correctional Facility), for nine months. I served my time at the State Farm just as I did the many times I was detained at the juvenile detention center. I frequently played table games and sports. I made a few futile attempts to attend school, but since I never took education seriously, I always ended up transferring to some prison job until my release date.

I eventually returned to the Indiana State Farm two more times by the time I turned nineteen. I returned on a theft charge the second time on a sentence of six months, and served another six months for assault and battery on a police officer in addition to resisting arrest. I continued to serve my prison time in the same manner by playing table games and sports but absolutely no school. By this time, I had become addicted to heroin.

By the time, I turned twenty-one my heroin addiction had caused my criminal conduct to escalate into serious felonies. In 1972, I was convicted by a jury, in criminal court for assault and battery with intent to commit a felony (robbery) and sentenced for one-to-ten years to a maximum-security prison, the Indiana State Reformatory (currently Pendleton Correctional Facility). Again, I served my prison time the same way I had served it many times before at the juvenile center and the State Farm. I was released from prison in 1975 after serving three years. However, since nothing had changed for the better inside my mind, I returned to the same environment and migrated to the same caliber of people who abused heroin, cocaine and committed serious crimes to support their habits.

Sometime in 1977, a jury convicted me in criminal court on a theft charge for being in possession of a stolen, $4,000 lady's diamond watch. I was not sentenced to any prison time. However, I received a $4,000 fine, which I did not have to pay because I was adjudicated as indigent. I immediately resumed my cycle of negative behaviors, committing more crimes to support my heroin addiction until my next arrest.

It is important for me to note here that my encounters with law enforcement and the court system were far more numerous in reality than what appears on the record. A number of times I was arrested and charged as a juvenile, but due to insufficient evidence the charges were subsequently dropped or the judge entered a judgment of not guilty. I was suspected or arrested with even more frequency as an adult, but my criminal aptitude by then was so advanced in relation to the insignificant world in which I lived that authorities found it nearly impossible to incarcerate me forever as they would have liked. In order to get me under control, the authorities ultimately used the habitual offender statute to exact more punishment on me than my petty crimes deserved. The bulk of crimes I committed were more a nuisance than a threat to society. I say this not to minimize the fact that my behavior was criminal, but the state and federal governments have created degrees of criminality from petty to severe as well as punishments consistent with the degree of the offense. Those sentencing guidelines were practically ignored in my case.

I had turned 28 when I found myself on November 30, 1979, my father's birthday, standing before another criminal court judge. On that day, I was sentenced to two years in prison after being convicted by a jury for possession of one gram of heroin. I was subsequently sentenced to an additional 30 years for being found to be a habitual offender simply because I had previously been convicted in 1972 and 1977 for two other felonies for which I had already received punishment. In essence, I was punished for the new crime, and then, punished all over again for two previous crimes.

I began serving my prison time the same way I had all my previous sentences. Outwardly, among the prison population, I projected a nonchalant attitude in relation to my 32-year prison sentence just as I had done while serving time on previous charges. But inwardly, this 32-year prison sentence had a totally different effect on my psyche. This time I would not be biding my time for a couple of years playing table games and sports before I would be free again soon. To the contrary, those 32 years felt like a "life sentence" or a "death sentence" depending which way one chooses to look at it. Of course, the Indiana Department of Correction allows every offender to receive one day's credit time for each day served if the offender manages to stay in the "privileged" time-class one status, by not violating prison rules, while incarcerated. Therefore, on a 32-year sentence an inmate could receive half time off and be released after serving 16 years. But it is not that simple. Sixteen years in prison is a mighty long, long, long time in a highly stressful and dangerous environment, and any new troubles inside prison walls could potentially add more time to my sentence.

There was, however, one positive experience I had with illicit drugs while in prison that set things in motion for my positive transformation. My mother had developed some form of throat cancer in 1981, and the doctors had surgically placed a trachea in her throat to relieve her of some complications and discomforts of breathing in hopes of prolonging her life. My mother was a devout Christian, and I have never known her to use tobacco, alcohol, drugs, or even profanity. I was taken aback by her development of cancer because I had assumed that mainly smokers developed that disease. By that time, I had been smoking cigarettes for about 18 years, but my mother's development of cancer influenced me in November 1981 to stop smoking cigarettes and using intravenous drugs. I understood nonetheless that it would be highly improbable for me to totally refrain from consuming some addictive substances in one night when in fact I had an extensive history of addictive behaviors. So I gave up tobacco and hard narcotics and returned to smoking marijuana. I never liked the effects marijuana had on me during my teenage years, so I knew that I would be smoking marijuana only seldom. I also realized that when I reached the point where I did not want to smoke marijuana any longer, I would have little difficulty weaning myself off it.

One evening in 1982, while confined to my one-man prison cell, I experienced a very strange phenomenon while under the intoxicating effects of marijuana. This experience occurred while I was incarcerated at the Indiana State Reformatory in Pendleton, Indiana. I was housed in H-Cellhouse, in cell 13, and on range 5B. Jerry Turentine was one of my next-door neighbors at that time in cell 14 on 5B. The steel bars, were about six inches apart, in that housing unit. It is quite easy for offenders next door to one another to stick an arm out of their cell and reach around the bars into the cell next door.

Jerry stuck his hand over into my cell one evening and whispered an offer to take a few hits off the "joint" he held in his hand. The marijuana cigarette or "joint" was already lit and slowly burning in his hand when I retrieved it. As customary for me before I take a draw off any "joint," I asked Jerry, "What number would you rate this "weed?" The prison culture had created a universal standard of 1 to 10 (10 being the higher potency) for measuring the potency of illicit drugs. Jerry already knew that I had a preference for smoking "weed" with a rating around 6 or 7 because anything higher would drive me out of my mind. I was afraid of marijuana that contained substantial potency. Sometimes even weak "weed" could get me "high," and I preferred to smoke a weaker strength than to smoke anything around 8 or 9, and definitely not 10. Jerry told me that the "weed" was about a 6 or 7, and I believed him because he had always been pretty straight with me during our eighteen months as neighbors. So, assuming that the joint Jerry had given me was about what I usually smoked, I took several long draws on it to insure that I achieved at least a decent "high" and then passed it back to Jerry. Very soon, something inside my head impelled me to quickly sit on the side of my bed or risk losing the ability to stand. I was urged to focus my attention on the gray steel wall opposite my bed only three feet away. The gray wall mysteriously turned into a video screen; then images and events of my past began to appear on the screen in an endless succession.

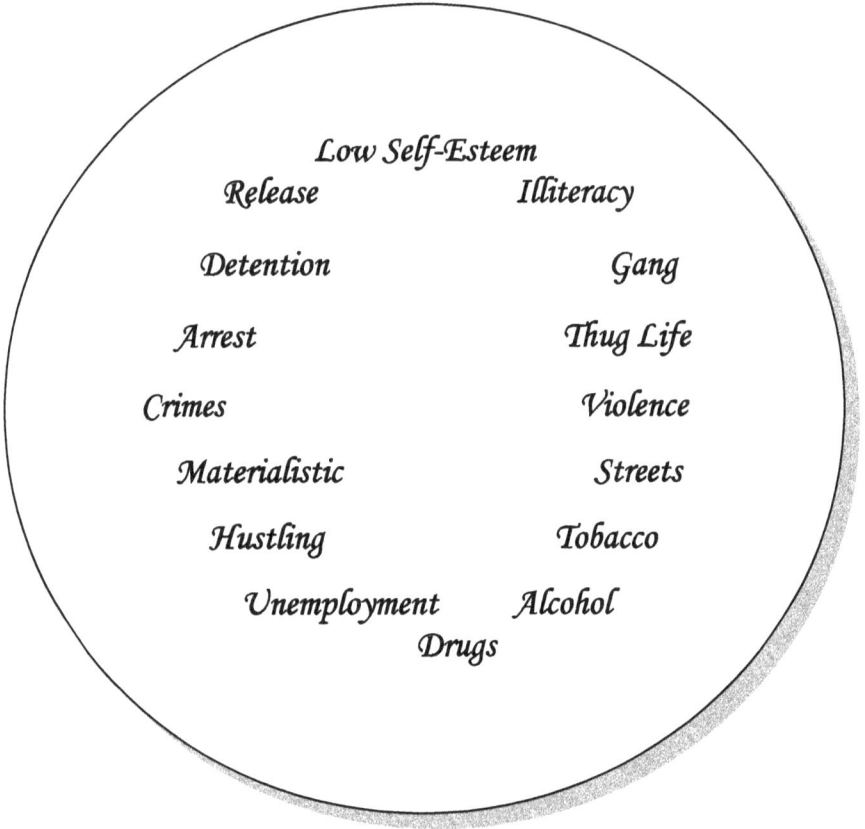

Low Self-Esteem

Release   Illiteracy

Detention   Gang

Arrest   Thug Life

Crimes   Violence

Materialistic   Streets

Hustling   Tobacco

Unemployment   Alcohol

Drugs

Chapter 13

The Positive Transformation

I know I am not crazy. Or am I? I could not believe what I was witnessing right before my eyes in my prison cell. This phenomenon could not be happening. No way in the world could it be real. And if it were real, it could not be happening to me.

Weird and strange phenomena happen to other people, I thought to myself. But there actually appeared to be a movie screen that mysteriously manifested on the wall of my cell. On this screen appeared images and events of my past life as brief film clips in an endless succession, something like the film clip technique that HBO uses to visually inform viewers what movies will be shown during the week or month. There also appeared to be a movie projector in my cell responsible for the projection of the very bright light on my cell wall. I had never experienced anything like that in my life. I did not know what to do. I did not know whether to stay and face whatever was to come of it or run to escape it. I realized, however, that running away from it was not an option since I was actually confined inside this cell and lacked the ability to exit it without the prison guard unlocking the door to the cell. I found this phenomenon confusing and frightening. I really did not know how to deal with it at first. But, eventually I had to accept that whatever it was, I needed to deal with it because it was not stopping or going anywhere, and I could not go anywhere because I was locked in that cell.

So I began to stare intently into that movie screen to observe what it had to show me. As I stated earlier, it was like watching brief film clips of situations from my past. Each clip seemed to last only a second or two, and then the next immediately followed. These clips provided just enough information to stimulate my memory concerning individual situations in the past. I began to realize, after viewing the clips, that I saw terrible or evil incidents from my past. Some instances were even against family members. The film clips moved on, reflecting past incidents that involved me committing sometimes, horrific acts against other people. I also began to realize that all these awful incidents were vile, even to my own conscience. I could not understand how and why these scenes were being reflected on the wall for me to review. First, I knew there could not be a movie projector in my cell. Second, I knew that I was not responsible for those projections on my wall because I had intentionally buried those shameful memories in the deepest recesses of my subconscious mind so that my conscience and soul would never again have to suffer the shame, guilt, and pain I experienced when I acknowledged the vile content of those memories.

Those projections could not have come from some carnal part of me because my vanity and ego would have preferred that those past vile acts remain submerged deep in the recesses of my memory so that the shame, guilt, and pain would lay dormant in my soul. Those projections, I decided, must have emanated from a spiritual essence inside me. Nonetheless, whether they derived from a carnal or spiritual part of me, I ultimately determined that they had to come from only me because there was no other tangible entity or machine in my cell, no projection equipment.

Most religious people would assume that the spiritual essence of a person is the Divine Source or God that lives within every human being, and though I was not seriously religious then, I came to that realization as I continued to review those brief film clips on the wall of my cell, one after another. I will detail here not all the vile acts the brief film clips conveyed to me, but only two examples of the scenes where I committed heinous acts against other people. The powerful effects of having to look at these and other similar scenes began what proved to be a positive transformation in my life.

One incident occurred between my younger brother Kermit "Ki Ki" Tinnin and me when we were around thirteen and fourteen years of age. We were in the kitchen of our parents' home. He and I had been having a disagreement about something petty earlier, and I had some water boiling on the stove for coffee. He wanted some of my hot water for his tea, but I vehemently refused to share the water with him, though there was plenty for both of us. When Ki Ki decided to take some of the water anyway, I grabbed the pot first and just threw the hot water in his chest causing serious burns to his chest and stomach. I instantly regretted what I had done and offered a sincere apology, but he would not accept it at that time. There was no blood, but the scalding water did cause top layers of his skin to peel. I became immensely grossed out by what I had done to my own brother, especially over something as simple and trivial as water that neither of us was paying for anyway. The fact that I had begun to experience that particular act all over again in that phantom movie theater only compounded the shame, guilt, and pain in my soul.

November 30, 1976, another incident occurred on my father's birthday. I was twenty-five and addicted to heroin. I armed myself with an unregistered firearm and went alone, during the early hours of the morning, to the home of a male acquaintance, Michael Thompson, who I suspected of dealing heroin, to rob him and anyone else in the home. Once I arrived in front of his home, I quietly approached the front door and abruptly kicked the door in and announced, "This is a stick up."

Since I was already familiar with the homeowners, I actually expected to find only two adults there at 8:30 a.m., the husband and wife. Ironically, on this particular occasion, the husband and wife were entertaining an unknown adult male visitor, and all three had risen frantically from their seats on the sofa and faced me as a result of the door being abruptly knocked open. Once I entered the home, I instantly realized that a second adult male was there and that a three or four-year-old boy was standing near me. I grabbed the little boy and held the gun on him to insure the adults' cooperation and eliminate the possibility of a challenge from the adult males. Nevertheless, I had miscalculated the bounty that I expected to find there and I came away with only a few fifty-dollar bags of heroin, at street value, and a few hundred dollars in cash but, more seriously, I had subjected others, including an innocent child, to grave danger.

When I got home where I lived with Karen Grundy and our daughters Stephanie, Cassandra and Joycelyn, I told Karen about the bold robbery I had committed at a suspected drug dealer's home and about my awful behavior of holding a gun on a child there as leverage to insure cooperation from the adult victims. I also shared with Karen and our daughters some of what I had stolen. As I placed cash in various envelopes designated for our household bills, my early Christian upbringing entered my thoughts concerning God's deadly wrath for certain transgressions, and I forewarned Karen that something bad would probably happen to me for what I had subjected that family to, especially the child.

The next day, December 1, 1976, which was also on my sister Pat's birthday, a day after I had held a child hostage with a gun and consequently to imminent danger, I approached another home armed with a gun. I intended to rob its occupants of drugs and money. I attempted to kick the door in but a sturdy chain latch prevented the door from opening beyond an inch or so. Then a second or two later a shot rang out from inside the home and subsequently a bullet passed through the door of the home and struck me in the right leg causing me to fall to the ground in the snow and breaking my right femur bone in half. I had attempted to break down the door of that home prior to being shot but this time I ended up in the hospital and subsequently in jail. The homeowner who shot me, however, never showed up in court, so it was another occasion where I escaped prosecution and punishment.

Reliving those experiences in my cell was enough for me. I did not want to view any more of those film clips of my past. My three most feared emotions, shame, guilt, and pain, were eating at my soul like cancer on a rapidly deteriorating lung. Shame, guilt, and pain inflicted the most excruciating torments on my soul as I continued to watch those film clips. I began to bargain with my spiritual self; I promised that if I were allowed to come down off this "high," I would never get "high" again.

Watching with horror those film clips of my awful history had "scared the day lights out of me" and had "put the fear of God in me." My soul urgently impelled my carnal self to earnestly question my spiritual self as to why it was compelling me to review my awful history. Though the response I received from my spiritual self was not audible, still the answer permeated my soul: "You are to take your awful experiences and share them with the youth of the world that they may not repeat the behaviors of your past." Then I thought that I was afraid to speak publicly in front of people because of my lack of knowledge, lack of vocabulary, and lack of education. My vocabulary then was primarily saturated with profanities to compensate for lack of standard language. My spiritual self then left me to figure out the obvious: "Education is the key."

I was not about to violate my word with the Divine Spirit that, in my opinion, lives inside every human being. Even if I did not understand anything else in life, I understood the omnipotence of the Spirit to withhold favor from the imbecile. So, once I descended from that artificial "high" and returned to my normal state of mind, I quickly organized a plan in my head designed to begin my journey to honor the commitment I had just made to my spiritual self.

First, I surrendered my favorite pastimes of playing table games and sports and placed them in a state of dormancy. Next, I promised to purchase a dictionary and borrow a newspaper from a fellow prisoner every day to start a regimen of teaching myself basic reading and writing skills for at least a year before enlisting in a formal GED program in the prison. Finally, I committed myself to refrain gradually from deviant behaviors, from the use of profanity and illicit drugs. At the same time, I was developing a positive demeanor and a positive attitude.

This new frame of thinking stimulated my memory to recall the time when I got into an intense argument with a longtime friend and fellow prisoner Samuel "Legs" Burton, who worked in the prison library. He was known for his extensive knowledge in a variety of subjects and for his superior intelligence. Inside our prison dormitory and in the presence of a number of other prisoners, we had argued fiercely about something insignificant, and at the conclusion of the argument, Legs in a disappointed and angry tone, shouted at me, "You're functionally illiterate and need to get your ass in school." That statement, especially coming from Legs, hurt and humiliated me. Legs thrust that statement through my heart, and it pierced deep in my soul because it was true and the real me was finally exposed to public scrutiny. I had always covered up the fact that I was illiterate by spewing an array of slang in conversations with others. I usually shared what knowledge I had gained from hearsay, and exhibited a flamboyant demeanor in the public.

After that experience in my cell with divine intervention, I approached Legs and humbly asked, "What books I should read?" The first book Legs provided me to read was Carter G. Woodson's *The Mis-education of the Negro*. When I finished that book and returned to Legs for a second book, he gave me *The Autobiography of Malcolm X* written together with Alex Haley.

The books "Mis-education of the Negro" and "The Autobiography of Malcolm X" collectively enlightened me and inspired me in many ways but most importantly taught me the power associated with knowledge. Being a disenfranchised and functionally illiterate young man, living powerless, was something that happened to be inherently part of my socio-economical status (indigent). Therefore, a sense of power was something that had eluded me all my life. However, when those two books helped me understand that power could be achieved through the acquisition of sufficient knowledge, simply by reading and meticulously studying the material one reads then the pursuit of more and more knowledge became a primary preoccupation for me.

"Mis-education of the Negro" in many ways, helped me understand the oppression of the descendants of Africans in America, the manipulation of history in textbooks by the white supremacy and the slave systems in America. This effectively indoctrinated the people subjugated by these formidable systems to accept their plight in this life as normal and that it was design by divine authority. That the people of African descent should not exert any unnecessary energy striving to overcome their sub-human station in life, particularly in America, and that the acquisition of professions like doctor, lawyer, professor, engineer, law enforcement or government official should be a farfetched prospect in the mind.

"Mis-education of the Negro" also teaches that an individual can free his or her self from the shackles of oppression and mental slavery through the acquisition of self-knowledge. I believe that it is stated somewhere in that book that: "The key to knowledge is the knowledge of self." I later discovered that very statement to be apparent in a number of other books I would eventually read and even articulated in public speeches by renowned personalities.

The book titled, "The Autobiography of Malcolm X" inspired me to believe that no matter how low in life a person may have descended, nevertheless, at some point the person can still raise his or her self up to prominence by making sound decisions and relying on positive influences. Also, positive reinforcements to transform one's character from vile to righteousness and that intense reading and studying can play a crucial role in achieving that kind of success.

In addition to the multitude of studies Malcolm undertook during his incarceration and subsequent freedom, he studied the entire dictionary to enhance his vocabulary and knowledge, thus the totality of his pursuit of knowledge, wisdom, and understanding culminated in him a very powerful and influential personality and shaped him into an iconic stature for historians. As a result of the convincing strategies contained in those two books on how to transform one's character from self-destruction and low self-esteem to one of righteousness and divine purpose, I incorporated into my life many of those strategies and especially a lot of the techniques Malcolm X used in reading and studying the dictionary.

I purchased a red medium-size *American Heritage Dictionary* for two packs of cigarettes from a fellow prisoner in

1982. I still have that dictionary today (June 28, 2010), which I save as a souvenir. I also purchased during that time many pencils, ink pens, and legal pads from the prison commissary that I used with that dictionary to define thousands of words from the newspapers I read every day. I wrote the words and their definitions on the legal pads so I could memorize them. My reading and writing skills were poor prior to taking up this self-imposed educational mission in 1982, and I therefore decided to develop my own literacy for at least a year before entering a GED program to lessen the difficulty of fitting into that program. My education level at that time was so inferior that it took me approximately four years to obtain my GED.

I suffered a temporary relapse of drug abuse for several months in 1985. This was probably because of my frustration and disappointment over losing the appeals of my criminal convictions. However, a number of the well-respected prisoners such as George Moon, William Moore-Bey, Marvin Hutcherson, Kevin Hill, and Darryl "Quarter Million" Jung personally expressed their disappointment with my spiraling out of control behavior.

Many of these guys and others even discouraged drug dealers within the prison population from doing business with me. This diligent and sincere concern influenced me to pull myself out of that mire and plunge deeper into studies of self, history, religion, and the law. I owe an immense amount of gratitude to these brothers and a few others whose names I am unable to recall at this time. I extend a very special thanks to Darryl "Quarter Million" Jung who passed away recently while still in prison before I had an opportunity to thank him publicly for the respect and generosity he always extended to me.

History has taught me that my ancestors (Africans) are the originators of civilization in the world and that they did not partake in self-destructive and addictive behaviors as I had done in my life. History that was reported accurately by well principled men and women about the innumerable contributions Africans made to civilization on the continent of Africa and all over the earth has made me aware in the words of the renowned Reverend Jesse Jackson that, "I am somebody." That awareness, which was sharply opposite to the degraded perception of African Americans conveyed by the Eurocentric indoctrination commonly taught as history to both European Americans and African Americans during the 1960s, 1950s and before, really made me feel good about myself and significantly elevated my self-esteem. I use the terms "African American" and "European American" when referring to people in America who are either of African descent or European descent since in fact I believe that God-Allah never made a Black person or a White person.

I am a member of the Moorish Science Temple of America, Inc. This is a religious organization of Moslems who practice the old time religion of Islamism and who abstain from calling people of African descent Negroes, Colored Folks, Black People or Ethiopians. "These names were given to slaves by slave holders in 1779 and lasted until 1865 during the time of slavery," according to Act 6 of the Divine Constitution and By-Laws of the Moorish Science Temple of America. Not only does the word "Black" allude to slavery but, in the teachings of Moorish Science, "Black according to science means death." Even in the book Rhetorical Criticism, at page 338, it is stated, in pertinent part, that: "[T]he means used to accomplish the act of memorializing the dead include the black color....." On the other hand, our Koran Questions for Moorish Children instruct us that "White means Purity, Purity means God and God means the Ruler of the Land." I am not aware of any human being capable of accurately claiming that title so therefore I refrain from attributing that title to any people. In fact, the concept of identifying people as Black or White seems to excessively cast the value of the one (Black) too low while the concept seems to excessively attribute value to the other (White) too high.

It seems that identifying the diverse Americans with a prefix denoting the continent of their ancestors, followed by hyphenated American gives every American a sense of equality as opposed to the terms "Black" and "White." Could not there be a sinister motive behind changing the identity of a people who were once identified as Africans or by their African tribal names (Bey or El) when they lived in Africa? However, it is common knowledge that the descendants of African slaves in America are products of forced migration to America, and these same people strangely came to be identified as Negroes, Colored Folks, Black People or Ethiopians? According to the teachings of Moorish Science, "Colored means anything that has been painted, stained, varnished or dyed," and that "Ethiopia means something divided." We of African descent are people of hue (color) and not Colored People. The complexion of our skin is an olive hue and range in varying degrees from very light to very dark, thus the term hue-man is derived.

It is also the teachings of Moorish Science that we, the Moors in America, define our nationality as Moorish-American "because we are descendants of Moroccans and born in America." We are direct relation to the Moors who had historically occupied the full extent of the northwestern and southwestern shores of Africa. Our race is defined as Asiatic. Thus, we are the children of Adam and Eve who were the mother and father of the hue-man family, Asiatic and Moslems. While the race of the Moors, as with other people of hue, is Asiatic and tied to the continent of Asia, the originators (Adam and Eve) of the hue-man family initially populated Asia and subsequently the rest of the world. Nevertheless, much of the Moorish culture is tied to the continent of Africa. This very analogy is true with European Americans whereas their race is actually defined as Caucasian while their European culture is tied to the sub-continent of Europe. However, the place of origin is Asia for the race of Caucasian and the root word "asia" is spelled out in that word. A reasonable research of the word "Caucasian" would undoubtedly substantiate its relationship to the continent of Asia and the common ancestors it shares with other Asiatic people.

Now, returning to the previous discussion concerning the degraded perception of African Americans. This was conveyed by the Eurocentric indoctrination commonly taught as history to both European Americans and African Americans during slavery in America to the 1960s. However, not all people of European descent believed those degraded perceptions. They all did not discriminate against Africans, African Americans, or other people of hue, nor did they agree with or embrace the slave system of Africans.

My historical studies revealed that European Americans like John Brown and his sons risked and lost their own lives opposing the slave system during the 1850s. Thousands of other European Americans assisted runaway slaves to escape through the Underground Railroad system. Many more European Americans and Jews risked and lost their lives aiding African Americans during the civil rights movement of the 1950s and 1960s.

To enhance my pursuit of positive transformation of my character during my incarceration and to bring my life in accordance to my recently adopted divine mission to uplift others and my belief in a Spiritual Authority of the universe, I joined the Moorish Science Temple of America in 1985. I discovered that this particular religious organization to be a perfect fit for me because of its emphasis in the study of "self" and its religious doctrine of "Islamism" in that members are taught that they are what their ancestors were and that the faith is practiced as the old time religion. The Moorish Science Temple of America espouses the divine principles of Love, Truth, Peace, Freedom, and Justice, which are the Five Highest Principles known to man. I have made these Five Highest Principles the foundation of my character. Prophet Noble Drew Ali is the founder of the Moorish Science Temple of America, which was founded in 1913 A.D. in Newark, New Jersey. The divine teachings of Prophet Noble Drew Ali are primarily responsible for resurrecting me from mental and spiritual death, planting my feet firmly within the bounds of righteousness, and raising my level of understanding about the omniscience, omnipotence, and omnipresence of God-Allah. In the divine lessons of Prophet Drew Ali, it teaches the Moors to love Jesus and to follow the teachings of Jesus. Prophet Noble Drew Ali teaches that all people of hue (color) are Asiatic including the natives of the African and Indian continents, and natives of the Orient, and natives of North, Central, and South America. Perhaps most importantly, he teaches that it is better to love than to hate. My primary calling is to follow in the footsteps of Prophet Noble Drew Ali by contributing to the uplift of fallen humanity, and whenever I am given an opportunity to share my awful history to discourage others from pursuing a self-destructive path in life then I am performing the uplifting principles of Prophet Noble Drew Ali. While the teachings of the Moorish Science Temple of America have redeemed my spirit from its "fallen stage of humanity" and thus caused it to gradually ascend to the highest plane of life with my heavenly Father God-Allah, still I am convinced that my feet are grounded in humility.

But those religious teachings were only part of the process that led to my transformation. I also studied the law closely and carefully to try to comprehend what had happened to me. The study of law taught me some of the legal mechanics the state of Indiana used to effectively imprison me for a long sentence and consequently the legal avenues available to extricate myself, pro se (self-representation), from imprisonment six months prior to my actual expiration date. I eventually experienced some personal measure of judicial vindication and success when I appeared back in court on December 8, 1994, on a pro se petition for post-conviction relief and the court granted me the relief that I sought. I was released from custody the next morning on December 9, 1994. However, I would not have been able to construct an effective pro se petition to present to the court and articulate a persuasive legal argument before the court without the blessings of Almighty God-Allah through the teachings of Noble Drew Ali's. Also, I could not do it without the benefit of a college education.

That education for me began with self-imposed education accompanied by the reading of newspapers from cover to cover, a dictionary, legal pads, and writing utensils. I earned my GED in four years. Then I moved on to the college level. By 1988 one of my European American friends, fellow prisoner Mark Coonan, aware that I had recently obtained my GED, urged me to continue my education by enrolling in the Ball State University college program. At that time, I had no real aspiration or confidence about higher education because of my lack of funds and what I perceived as my lack of aptitude. Mark worked in the college admissions office and assured me that he could assist me by securing me a Pell grant that would pay my college tuition and for my books. Furthermore, he encouraged me by telling me that I had as much ability to succeed as any other prisoner in the college program.

Despite his help and encouragement, I was still reluctant when I enrolled in the Ball State University college extension program for the upcoming fall semester of 1988. Nevertheless, I gradually made a smooth transition into the program and acclimated to the prospect of being college educated. Here, the idea of becoming educated for some in the African American community can be a very discouraging prospect because of a cultural perspective that aspirations of education is a "European American thing" or "trying to be like a European American person" and therefore is equated with an African American "selling out" one's toughness and African American culture. Nevertheless, I rose above that backwards brand of thinking, and overcame the notion that becoming educated was a form of "selling out" and thereby moved on with my educational aspirations.

To complement my educational and spiritual aspirations and to overcome my nervousness about public speaking, I selected a major in speech communications because it obviously entailed practice in public speaking. I definitely needed to become a proficient public speaker to articulate the lessons I had to impart to the youth of the world and to develop a platform to enact my public and spiritual ambitions.

By 1989, the prison where I was incarcerated blessed me with the opportunity to address groups of teen students who were bused to the prison to attend a "Scared Straight" program. A few of the teens had apparently shown signs of deviancy, and the authorities in their lives wanted to avert those counter-productive behaviors by "scaring them straight" with tough talks from persons currently incarcerated in a maximum security prison. This timely opportunity represented a significant ascension in my quest to address the youth of Indiana and neighboring states and consequently developed a platform from which to launch my public speaking aspirations.

Finally, every opportunity I am given to address a group or an individual and to use my awful history to discourage people from a destructive path in life inherently provides me with another opportunity to repent for the countless transgressions I perpetrated against other people and society as a whole. I was released from prison on December 9, 1994, and in the introduction of this book, I shared the many positive opportunities bestowed on me since my release, by numerous kind and forgiving business people, community leaders, law enforcement officials, politicians, clergy, educators, family, and friends. I give all praises to Allah and thank Him for intervening in my life and in the affairs of all the peoples of the earth.

PEACE

S. A., 2009 with Tony Dungy, Kim, Khadijah

S.A. pictured with Dr. Vernon G. Smith, Ind. State Rep. 1998

S.A. pictured with my former English professor, Stephen Guy, at his home in 2006 during his retirement party.

S.A. pictured with Judge Greg Mathis at a Teen Court session around 1998 in Indianapolis, Indiana.

S. A. pictured in 1997 with
Mavs' Award

S. A. receives Award from, Jerome
Moore & Bill West

S. A. 1999 & Darren Washington visit
Moors at Branchville C.F.

Donald "Eastside Don" Allen, Robert Earl Badelle, Wilbur "Face"
Graham, James Perry, Ronald Mason-Bey, Danny Graham, Leroy
Graves-El, Larry Owens, Robert Lewis McFarland, Ray Charles
Miller, Rodney Williams-Bey, S. A. Tinnin-Bey

S.A. 2003 Celebration with Moors at Branchville C.F.

S.A. 2003 Celebration with Moors at Pendleton C.F.

INDEX

Give a Gift to a
Friend or Family Member

CHECK YOUR FAVORITE BOOKSTORE OR ORDER NOW

☐ Yes, please send ____ copies of *Cycle / Psycho Personality* at $19.95 each, plus $5 shipping per book (Indiana residents please add 7% sales tax per book). Allow 14 days for delivery.

My check or money order is enclosed for the amount of $_____

My mailing address is:

Name: _____

Address: _____

City: _____ State: _____ Zip: _____

Telephone: _____

Email address: _____

Please make your check payable and return to:

Jo-Val Publishing
8485 Robin Run Way
Avon, Indiana 46123

Call for discounts on large orders
Call credit card orders to 1-317-272-1060
1-317-457-8752

Email: jo@jvpublishers.com
stinninbey@yahoo.com

Visit our website: www.jvpublishers.com
Author's page: www.jvpublisher.com/Cycle-Psycho-Personality.html

Author, S. A. Tinnin-Bey, was born in Indianapolis, Indiana where he continues to reside. Acquired a General Education Diploma at Indiana State Reformatory (Pendleton Correctional Facility), and then acquired an Associate of Arts Degree at Ball State University, in Muncie, Indiana. After years of encouragement from family and friends, this inspiring book, **"Cycle/Psycho Personality"** was created to encourage others to live a motivated and a successful happier life.

Tinnin-Bey offers motivational seminars for youth groups, churches, correctional centers and many other functions. For more information or to book a seminar, please contact him at: stinninbey@yahoo.com or 317-457-8752

www.ingramcontent.com/pod-product-compliance
Lightning Source LLC
Chambersburg PA
CBHW072247270326
41930CB00010B/2293